The Premier League is a peculiar beast.

Albion have progressed from obsessing about finishing in the top three to staying outside ...

This is the landscape for every club apart from the Big Six.

Even Everton in the early stages of the season, when Wayne Rooney snatched a point at the Amex with a last-gasp penalty, had genuine concerns about dropping into the Championship.

Albion know how tough it is to escape from the second tier. The Championship is an ultra-competitive grind, 46 games, a good number of them stamina-sapping treks north for players and supporters alike.

Would you really want to return to that?

Thirty-four years divided Albion's stints in the top flight of English football.

Having spent that long trying to get back, it would have been a shame if it had immediately gone to waste.

Remaining in the Premier League is, for a club of Albion's stature, as much of an achievement as getting there.

An alternative type of achievement, stirring relief rather than unbridled joy, but success all the same.

Chris Hughton's Albion have done it without abandoning their DNA.

The manager consistent as ever in his approach, level-headed in victory and defeat.

Yes, an influx of foreign signings spearheaded by Player of the Season Pascal Gross played a big part.

Survival was nevertheless underpinned by the club's ethos, a tight-knit bond in the dressing room and between players and supporters, everyone pushing in the same direction.

The longer Albion stay in the Premier League, the more difficult that will be to maintain. Improving the squad without losing that core spirit is an awkward balance, but that is a conversation for another occasion.

For now, celebrate securing a sixth season in the top flight. Be grateful for following one of the 20 best teams in the country.

And remember the Premier League is not quite as predictable as some would have you believe.

Who would have thought Albion would hit the 40-point mark with two matches to spare? Or that they would finish above established clubs like Stoke, relegated after a decade in the top flight?

And who would have thought Burnley will be hosting European opponents at Turf Moor next season?

Dreams do not die in the Premier League—they just take on a different dimension.

Andy Naylor
Chief Sports Reporter, The Argus

Albion's route

All things Brighton beautiful after Friday

IT ALWAYS looked like it could be a special season.

Exciting, challenging, a trip into unknown? All of those.

And, yes, depressing at times too when the going got tough and the results and goals dried up for a few weeks.

Wins were events and Albion had to be at their best to get them (with the exceptions of Watford at home and Swansea away).

But the highs were very high – and none more so than what we witnessed on Friday as safety was secured with favours from no one.

In The Prem today, Andy Naylor tracks the nine-month path to where Albion are this morning.

And Brian Owen, with help from the experts, plots how that big night against Manchester United was made possible.

It was an evening which will be cherished for decades.

And that in a part of the world which has plenty going for it.

The morning after the night before, Brighton and Hove didn't wake up with a hangover.

Well okay, some people did! But the city itself woke bright, early, full of life and colour and ready for the annual festival.

The city's streets buzzed and the seafront glistened.

That is a traditional event this time every May.

Brighton is the place to be, as the old advertising slogan used to say.

Premier League status in May? That's a first. But it sits very nicely in a special city.

This is how it was secured and maintained – both over the season and on the night.

TOP FLIGHT
THE SEAGULLS' FIRST SEASON IN THE PREMIER LEAGUE
ONLY £2.99
SPECIAL EDITION
AMERICAN EXPRESS
EVERY 2017/18 MATCH REPORT FROM *The Argus*

Don't miss our look back at the Albion Premier League campaign - coming just as soon as the season ends

Hardly a wrong turn on return to top flight

ALBION have achieved their goal of staying in the Premier League.

The Seagulls will be competing in the top flight of English football again next season for only the sixth time in their history.

Chief Sports Reporter ANDY NAYLOR looks back at how Chris Hughton's side secured safety.

AUGUST

An opening fixture against Manchester City at the Amex always looked tough. Just how tough became more transparent as the season progressed.

For 69 minutes, the team that eventually ran away with the title under Pep Guardiola were kept at bay.

Another more routine 2-0 defeat followed at 2015-16 champions Leicester.

No goals and no points became no goals and one point with a 0-0 draw at Watford against ten men for more than an hour after Miguel Britos nearly cut Anthony Knockaert in half. Welcome to the Premier League.

SEPTEMBER

The doom-mongers went back into hibernation. Pascal Gross hinted at how influential he would be with two goals in a first, convincing win at home to West Brom.

An away point or three beckoned as well at Bournemouth through Solly March. That was until the Cherries turned it around and evergreen predator Jermain Defoe popped up with the winner.

Back-to-back home victories came at a price for Tomer Hemed, scorer of the only goal against Newcastle. Retrospectively suspended by the FA for treading on DeAndre Yedlin, the Israeli striker was destined from then on to play second fiddle to Glenn Murray.

OCTOBER

The first away test against one of the Big Six was negotiated satisfactorily in a 2-0 defeat at Arsenal, considering Chris Hughton's lack of striking options forced him to use Izzy Brown as a false No.9.

Wayne Rooney's last-gasp equaliser in a 1-1 draw for Everton at the Amex felt like a waste, the same outcome against Southampton less so after falling behind early.

In-between, Murray's double and the first eye-catching contribution from Jose Izquierdo in a 3-0 romp

Lewis Dunk celebrates after scoring against Arsenal

away to West Ham was a huge breakthrough.

NOVEMBER

Too good to be true, surely? Albion entered the third international break in ninth with successive away wins, courtesy of Murray at Swansea.

On the resumption, an eventful 2-2 draw at home to Stoke, coming from behind twice, was followed by one of the best performances of the season in defeat by a single goal against Manchester United at Old Trafford.

The first top flight clash since 1981 with bitter rivals Crystal Palace fell flat. An uneventful 0-0 draw

remained in the memory only due to complaints from the away supporters about the conduct of Sussex Police.

DECEMBER

The final month of 2017 looked difficult on paper, seven games squeezed into 29 days.

That is the way it panned out as Liverpool at home, Spurs and Chelsea away, produced three defeats, one goal and nine conceded.

Five of them came in a harsh home drubbing as Jurgen Klopp's side exhibited their counter-attacking prowess.

A horrible display at Huddersfield and a wasteful home deadlock

with Burnley, including a missed penalty by Murray, was followed by the relief of a first victory in seven against Watford just before Christmas.

A memorable year ended with a useful point at Newcastle.

JANUARY

The danger of relegation grew. Two more home points slipped away after leading twice against Bournemouth. A lifeless performance at West Brom brought an end to skipper Bruno's place in the team for a while.

Replacement Ezequiel Schelotto was denied a penalty in the second home drubbing of the season, 4-0

to Premier survival

Opening day against Man City

Jose Izquierdo lets fly

Glenn Murray at West Ham

Pascal Gross, right, celebrates with Anthony Knockaert the goal that secured Albion's Premier League status

Premier League							
Man City (C)	36	30	4	2	102	26	94
Man Utd	36	24	5	7	67	28	77
Liverpool	37	20	12	5	80	38	72
Tottenham	36	21	8	7	68	32	71
Chelsea	36	21	6	9	61	34	69
Arsenal	36	18	6	12	72	48	60
Burnley	37	14	12	11	35	37	54
Everton	37	13	10	14	43	55	49
Leicester	36	11	11	14	49	54	44
Newcastle	36	11	8	17	36	46	41
Crystal Palace	37	10	11	16	43	55	41
Bournemouth	37	10	11	16	43	60	41
Watford	37	11	8	18	44	63	41
ALBION	36	9	13	14	33	47	40
West Ham	36	9	11	16	45	67	38
Huddersfield	36	9	9	18	27	56	36
Southampton	36	6	15	15	36	55	33
Swansea	36	8	9	19	27	53	33
West Brom	37	6	13	18	31	54	31
Stoke	37	6	12	19	33	67	30

by Chelsea, although the scoreline again did not reflect Albion's spirit.

They were too close for comfort to the drop zone at that stage, just two points and two places. Record buy Jurgen Locadia and Leo Ulloa were both on board to bolster Hughton's attacking options as the transfer window and month closed with an important point at fellow strugglers Southampton.

FEBRUARY

A pivotal return to winning form after six matches without one. West Ham were convincing victims again, a game featuring Izquierdo's Goal of the Season.

Mathew Ryan made a vital late penalty save from Charlie Adam to deprive Stoke of a much-needed victory after Izquierdo's team Goal of the Season (we've awarded that ourselves).

An emphatic double completed over Swansea as well, rounded off by Locadia and also featuring a fourth own goal for the outstanding Lewis Dunk.

MARCH

No points against the top six became three as Arsenal were despatched by Murray and Dunk at the Amex in a memorable victory.

Three wins in a five-match unbeaten sequence allowed some leeway for another awkward period.

The 2-0 defeat at Everton ranked alongside those at Huddersfield and West Brom in performance terms, while Leicester's smash and grab at the Amex ensured the trapdoor was still a little too close for comfort.

APRIL

Palpable anxiety at the Amex for the first time as another lead is frittered away against Huddersfield by an uncharacteristic Shane Duffy error.

Mistakes galore at, of all places, Selhurst Park in the opening 25 minutes a week later lead to defeat by the odd goal in five.

The failings of others at the bottom continue to sustain the cush-ion. Bruno is restored and, three days after the Palace setback, Spurs are held. The performance was invigorating, considering the quality of the opposition and their formidable away record.

A hard-earned point at Burnley and a first clean sheet of the year edges Albion closer.

MAY

The perfect finale. A 1-0 win over Manchester United at a packed-out Amex, 36 years after the only previous victory against the Red Devils by the same margin, clinches survival with two games to spare.

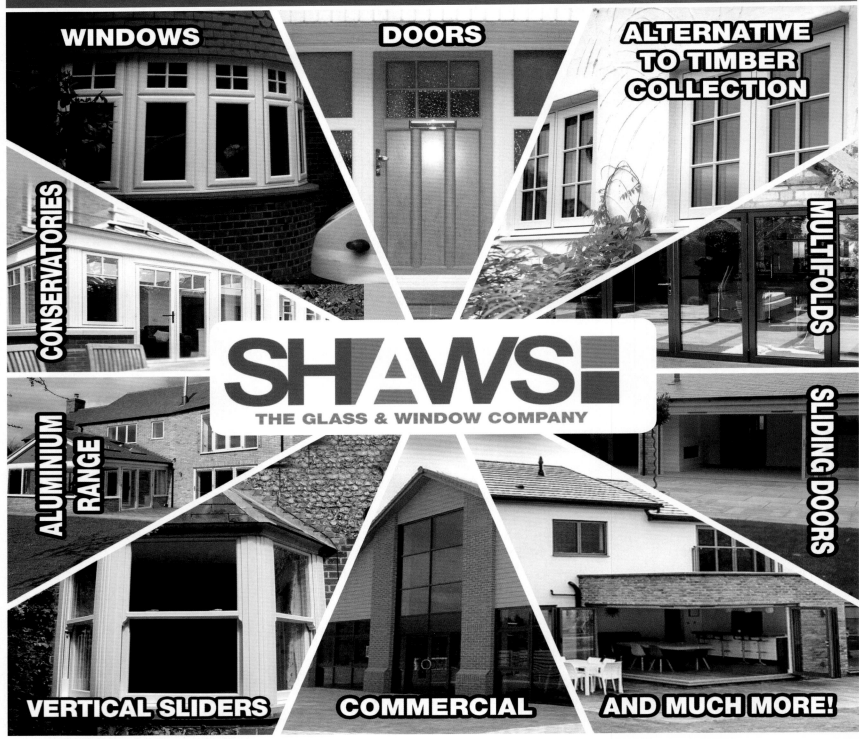

THE MEETING PLACE CAFE, OPEN AIR CAFE BY THE SEA

Supporting Brighton and Hove Albion in the Premier league
On the boundary of Brighton & Hove - Kingsway/ Kings Road BN3 2WN

01273 206417

For reservation call Emilio or Roberto
on **01273 325014** or
bookings@theregencyrestaurant.co.uk
131 Kings Road, Brighton, BN1 2HH
www.theregencyrestaurant.co.uk

THE OLDEST SEAFOOD RESTAURANT ON BRIGHTON SEAFRONT.

Experience
enticing flavours of locally caught fresh fish, whilst enjoying spectacular views of the English Channel, the i360 and the West Pier.

Albion ratings ✓

MATHEW RYAN
Excellent reflexes to keep out point-blank header from Jesus in first half. Dunk's was through him quickly for City's second goal. **7**

BRUNO
Adapted comfortably to the level. Helped by March, the veteran Spanish skipper made sure he was never exposed for pace. **7**

SHANE DUFFY
Solid apart from underhit back-pass in second half which Aguero should have punished. Nearly broke the deadlock with a shot. **7**

LEWIS DUNK
Sound as well after Jesus left him for dead once early on. A threat at set-plays, including a double effort from a corner. **7**

MARKUS SUTTNER
Steady debut from the Austrian. Will have more opportunities in other matches to demonstrate the quality of his delivery. **7**

SOLLY MARCH
Among the Albion players who looked comfortable in such company. Was at ease on the ball, maybe a bit much so on one occasion, but too much of it had to be in his own half. **7**

Albion boss has a quick Pep talk with his Man City counterpart

DALE STEPHENS
Involved in a lot of chasing, closing down and blocking of passing options. But a loss of possession was costly. **6**

DAVY PROPPER
Gave the ball away too easily on a couple of glaring first-half occasions but was better when he kept the passing simple. Improved after break. **5**

IZZY BROWN
Signs were promising but was not on for long enough to make an impact. Gave a glimpse of how he can beat a man and get stuck in. **5**

PASCAL GROSS
Precious little seen of the man brought to link midfield with attack. Flighted a precise free-kick for Dunk to head towards goal. **5**

TOMER HEMED
Chosen to plough the lone furrow in attack and struggled to get into the game or close down the City back three as they played the ball out. **5**

SUBS
Jamie Murphy: Got into some good positions but nothing really came of them. **5**
Glenn Murray: On for Hemed to lead line. **5**
Knockaert: Was waiting to go on when City scored their second. Added a good outlet.

Plucky Albion

Hughton's game-plan undone by late double

 Albion..........0
 Man City......2

ALBION'S first match in the Premier League was against the side who, in all probability, will finish the season in first place.

That is the context for a plucky defeat which obeyed the script with one exception.

It took Pep Guardiola's title favourites 70 minutes to find a way through, thanks to the pragmatism and organisational skills of Chris Hughton which will serve the Seagulls well in the challenges ahead.

Playing with two strikers, as Albion did in the Championship, or adopting a front-foot approach would have been suicide against a team of City's quality.

They would have been picked off and beaten heavily. The players followed the orders, kept their discipline and shape, and emerged with credit confronting landslide odds.

Either side of the two goals in five minutes which provided a realistic reflection of City's superiority, Guardiola introduced Leroy Sane, Raheem Sterling and Bernardo Silva from a bench costing more to assemble than the Amex and the lavishly equipped training complex in Lancing.

Hughton said: "Somebody did tell me that and when you put it that way it sounds incredibly strange, but if I was in his (Guardiola's) shoes I'd be doing exactly the same.

"Apart from good quality players, they've bought really good legs. If I look at the three full-backs (Kyle Walker, Danilo and Benjamin Mendy) they are all strong, quick, athletic. The way they play that's obviously what they wanted."

There will be an element of relief for Hughton that Albion were not slayed. "You can never say it's a concern, because you never go into the game thinking that," he said.

"But I've been on the end of good results against the top teams at home and also some really tough ones. It can happen. If they get their first goal earlier in the game, then the second one, then it can be.

"Fortunately for us we didn't allow that to happen and for the majority of the game we were right in it."

They were because Hughton's players stuck to the instructions and because they defended heroically. No other team matched Albion's 42 clearances on the opening

A shaven-headed David Silva is fouled by Dale Stephens and, below, Sergio Aguero celebrates his goal

By ANDY NAYLOR
Chief sports reporter

weekend.

The only justifiable criticism was a looseness with the 22% of the possession they had – it felt like considerably less.

Hughton said: "You work before the game and have a plan, sometimes they get it right and sometimes they don't. You can't be expansive against the quality they've got. Probably the one negative was when we had periods we could have kept the ball a bit better, but they pressed very well.

"They have in the side, apart from great quality, a lot of energy as well. He (Guardiola) has got them pressing very well and it's hard to get around that press. Overall I was certainly pleased with the game plan."

While Walker was more like a right-winger than right wingback for City and Guardiola could afford to sacrifice Danilo for Sane in search of the breakthrough, Solly March was forced to operate more like a right-back.

March drew appreciative ap-

plause for beating two City players deep inside his own territory on one occasion in the first half. He looked comfortable at the level, as did the defensive unit.

They will be Albion's strength. The weakness, certainly at the moment until the attacking transfer business is completed, is pace through the middle.

Although the Premier League is packed with attacking quality, the Seagulls will not face a more severe examination in their remaining 37 tests than a quartet of David Silva and Kevin De Bruyne behind Sergio Aguero and Gabriel Jesus.

Silva, now shaven-headed, is

make City dig deep

Albion skipper Bruno wins a header against Manchester City frontman Jesus at the Amex in the Premier League opener.

Pictures: Simon Dack

the teams

Albion (4-4-1-1): Ryan; Bruno, Dunk, Duffy, Suttner; March, Propper, Stephens, Brown; Gross; Hemed.

Subs: Murphy for Brown (23), Murray for Hemed (60), Knockaert for March (75), Maenpaa, Huenemeier, Rosenior, Sidwell.

Goals: None.

Red cards: None.

Yellow cards: None.

Man City (3-5-2): Ederson; Kompany, Otamendi, Stones; Walker, Fernandinho, De Bruyne, D.Silva, Danilo; Jesus, Aguero.

Subs: Sane for Danilo (68), Sterling for Jesus (77), B. Silva for Aguero (82), Bravo, Mangala, Toure, Foden.

Goals: Aguero (70), Dunk own goal (75).

Red cards: None.

Yellow cards: Jesus (29) deliberate handball, Sterling (82) foul.

Referee: Michael Oliver.

Attendance: 30,415 (3,025).

match stats

ALBION		MAN CITY
2	Shots on target	4
4	Shots off	10
3	Corners	10
3	Offsides	1
6	Free-kicks conceded	9

ref watch

The impressive Michael Oliver was spot on to rule out Gabriel Jesus's goal for handball and got great support from assistant Simon Bennett on a tight offside against David Silva after the break. **8**

next up

Leicester City v Albion, Premier League, Saturday (3pm).

and table

Premier League

	P	W	D	L	F	A	Pts
Man Utd	1	1	0	0	4	0	3
Huddersfield	1	1	0	0	3	0	3
Man City	1	1	0	0	2	0	3
Tottenham	1	1	0	0	2	0	3
Arsenal	1	1	0	0	4	3	3
Burnley	1	1	0	0	3	2	3
Everton	1	1	0	0	1	0	3
West Brom	1	1	0	0	1	0	3
Liverpool	1	0	1	0	3	3	1
Watford	1	0	1	0	3	3	1
Southampton	1	0	1	0	0	0	1
Swansea	1	0	1	0	0	0	1
Leicester	1	0	0	1	3	4	0
Chelsea	1	0	0	1	2	3	0
Bournemouth	1	0	0	1	0	1	0
Stoke	1	0	0	1	0	1	0
ALBION	1	0	0	1	0	2	0
Newcastle	1	0	0	1	0	2	0
Crystal Palace	1	0	0	1	0	3	0
West Ham	1	0	0	1	0	4	0

City's gold, a sublime creator. His slide-rule pass after Dale Stephens was dispossessed on halfway by De Bruyne was tucked away by Aguero, his 16th goal in his last 18 games.

Silva now has 58 Premier League assists since 2011-12, at least 15 more than any other player, a symbol of his enduring influence.

Aguero was not going to miss a second time after wasting a gift when Shane Duffy duffed a back-pass, the only blemish of a strong performance by the Irishman.

The hand of Jesus, via his chest, was well spotted by referee Michael Oliver in the first half as he latched onto an exquisite ball from De Bruyne. It was disallowed and the Brazilian was booked as he received treatment. Mathew Ryan increased the frustration with a wonderful save from a point-blank header which Jesus should have dispatched.

The persistent threat from Jesus induced the own goal from Lewis Dunk, which sealed Albion's fate. Dunk, like partner Duffy otherwise a tower of strength, was the wrong side of Jesus as he directed a header from Fernandinho's cross through the arms of a surprised Ryan.

Albion's central defenders offered their best hope of scoring from set-plays, the one area where City looked unconvincing.

At 0-0 Duffy had a shot from a corner deflected just wide. From the corner that followed, dropped by the unemployed Ederson, Dunk had successive efforts blocked before Davy Propper's drive whistled wide.

While the Dutchman's debut alongside Stephens was a real mixed bag, Hughton's stifling plot was not helped by losing the energy and athleticism of another of the new signings, Chelsea loanee Izzy Brown, to a hamstring injury midway through the first half.

Brown's replacement, Jamie Murphy, had an 'if only' moment just before the break. Albion might have led if the Scot had been able to take a crossfield pass from Stephens in his stride when fleetingly goal side of Walker.

The Premier League's other Albion are up next at the Amex next month. The transfer window will be shut by then and they will also have visited Leicester and Bournemouth. This period will be a more realistic guide to the survival aspirations than City. Facing them first might be a blessing in disguise. Once the rust is removed and City are in full stride, future opponents may wish for more grounds like Guardiola's spiritual home, Barcelona's Nou Camp, which has a chapel beside the walkway to the pitch.

Albion ratings ✓

MATHEW RYAN
Came out sharply to poke the ball away from clean-through Vardy but was playing catch-up from the first minute after failing to hold Mahrez's shot.
 5

BRUNO
Looks at home in this company. Has the poise and first touch to set moves rolling. One criticism - giving away dangerous free-kicks.
7

LEWIS DUNK
Another big test and Albion generally marshalled Vardy well in central areas, although Okazaki playing off him was more of a handful.
7

SHANE DUFFY
Saw Maguire get above him for the second goal but also did some decent stuff, notably blocking from Vardy right in front of goal.
7

MARKUS SUTTNER
An unhappy time, especially in the first half. Let Mahrez coast inside him far too easily for the opener.
 5

SOLLY MARCH
Glimmers in both halves that he might fashion an opening. Involved in most of Albion's best moments.
 7

Skipper Bruno applauds the travelling fans at the King Power stadium

DALE STEPHENS
Tidy enough. Most of his best work was in deep areas, although cross set up shooting chance for Murphy.
6

DAVY PROPPER
Let-off when caught in possession by Ndidi. Will have to get used to the pace of the English game. Disciplined without the ball.
 6

JAMIE MURPHY
Got the nod over Knockaert. Scot had first-half shot blocked. No real penetration, initially down right, then left.
 6

PASCAL GROSS
Looked off the pace in the No.10 role. Free-kicks were not the best either. Replaced soon after second goal.
 5

GLENN MURRAY
Had to feed off scraps. Just offside when hooking in March's reverse pass in first half. Failed to connect from same supply line before hobbling off.
 6

SUBS
ANTHONY KNOCKAERT: On for second game running at 0-2. No chance to shine against former club.
TOMER HEMED: 20-yard shot forced Schmeichel into rare save.

No surprises yet

Fleet-footed Foxes are a benchmark for Albion

 Leicester.....2
 Albion.........0

NO points, no goals, no surprise.

That is a realistic assessment two games into Albion's quest for Premier League survival.

Manchester City at home and Leicester away were always going to be tough assignments.

Tougher than those faced by Crystal Palace and Bournemouth, who are both far more established and yet have suffered the same fate.

Safety will almost certainly hinge on a healthy number of wins at the Amex against teams in the bottom half and scrapping for points here and there on the road.

In terms of the latter, Albion will have to improve considerably on what they produced at the King Power Stadium.

Their work in the transfer window is not finished, which is just as well.

Chris Hughton and the recruitment team are well aware – and have been from day one – that more pace is needed through the middle in attacking areas to cause discomfort to opposing defences.

It is a difficult and expensive position to fill as they continue to beaver away at a list of similar targets, including Cardiff's Kenneth Zohore and Everton's Oumar Niasse.

Leicester, aside from their shock title success of two seasons ago, are several years ahead of where Albion eventually want to be.

The difference in experience and quality showed in a comprehensive defeat. The home side were never required to move out of second gear.

Hughton said: "I know how tough it is and, if anything, if I look at my experiences before it's probably even tougher now.

"But I certainly believe there are a big group of teams outside of that top six. That doesn't mean we can't get points from those top six but realistically our points are going to be against the teams out of that top six and the experience we get from defeats like this have to make us better.

"It's trying to get to that level and aspire to be what Leicester are. If you take out the season in the middle when they were exceptional, of course, they have become a very consistent and strong Premier League team.

"If I look at the way they do it, generally it's a form of 4-4-2. They know what they are good at and

Harry Maguire rises highest to put Leicester 2-0 up and, below, Shane Duffy thwarts Jamie Vardy

By ANDY NAYLOR
Chief sports reporter

they have taken the qualities they had from the Championship into the Premier League and improved it by better players.

"Nobody expected the season

before last they had. That stands them above Burnley, Bournemouth, Watford that have come up and stayed up but they have done it in a way that suits the club.

"They have a philosophy, a way of playing, that hasn't veered too much and it's a good example for anyone."

It helps when you have the rapid Riyad Mahrez weaving magic and a poacher like Shinji Okazaki playing off the electric Jamie Vardy.

Leicester had no need for £25 million signing Kelechi Iheanacho, absent from the squad with a toe injury. It will be a gradual process for Albion to acquire similar talent.

It is still very early days for their new signings, who were collectively found wanting.

Mathew Ryan and Markus Suttner were culpable when Okazaki pounced after just 52 seconds. In midfield, Davy Propper faces an

but it must get better

Mathew Ryan punches under pressure in a crowded Albion penalty area. Pictures: Richard Parkes

the teams

Albion (4-4-1-1): Ryan; Bruno, Duffy, Dunk, Suttner; March, Stephens, Propper, Murphy; Gross; Murray.
Subs: Knockaert for Gross (63), Hemed for Murray (66), Bong, Huenemeier, Skalak, Maenpaa, Rosenior.
Goals: None.
Red cards: None.
Yellow cards: None.
Leicester (4-4-1-1): Schmeichel; Simpson, Morgan, Maguire, Fuchs; Mahrez, James, Ndidi, Albrighton; Okazaki; Vardy.
Subs: Slimani for Okazaki (76), Gray for Vardy (90), Chilwell, King, Hamer, Amartey, Ulloa.
Goals: Okazaki (1), Maguire (55).
Red cards: None.
Yellow cards: Morgan (50) foul.
Referee: Lee Probert.
Attendance: 31,902.

match stats

ALBION		LEICESTER
2	Shots on target	3
4	Shots off	10
2	Corners	6
1	Offsides	1
10	free-kicks conceded	8
55	Possession	45

Glenn Murray gets treatment

ref watch

It was a trouble-free game for Lee Probert and he came through it comfortably. Was he a touch kind to the Seagulls when blowing for full-time as Mahrez ran clean through on goal? **7**

next match

Albion v Barnet, Carabao Cup second round, tomorrow (7.45pm).

and table

Premier League

	P	W	D	L	F	A	Pts
Man Utd	2	2	0	0	8	0	6
Huddersfield	2	2	0	0	4	0	6
West Brom	2	2	0	0	2	0	6
Watford	2	1	1	0	5	3	4
Liverpool	2	1	1	0	4	3	4
Southampton	2	1	1	0	3	2	4
Man City	1	1	0	0	2	0	3
Leicester	2	1	0	1	5	4	3
Tottenham	2	1	0	1	3	2	3
Everton	1	1	0	0	1	0	3
Arsenal	2	1	0	1	4	4	3
Chelsea	2	1	0	1	4	4	3
Burnley	2	1	0	1	3	3	3
Stoke	2	1	0	1	1	1	3
Swansea	2	0	1	1	0	4	1
Bournemouth	2	0	0	2	0	3	0
Newcastle	2	0	0	2	0	3	0
ALBION	2	0	0	2	0	4	0
Crystal Palace	2	0	0	2	0	4	0
West Ham	2	0	0	2	2	7	0

adjustment in intensity from Dutch football.

Pascal Gross, who has made an encouraging impact in the No.10 role, looked pedestrian on this occasion and was substituted.

The four players who have coped most effectively with the step up so far across the two games have been Bruno, Lewis Dunk, Shane Duffy and Solly March.

Conceding inside the opening minute away from home in prevent-able fashion is a cardinal sin at any level. Mahrez beat Suttner far too easily on the inside. The shot went through a crowd of players, but Ryan should have dealt with it better than spilling a tap-in for Okazaki.

The goal stemmed initially from an Albion attack. Leicester, even at home, tend to play more like an away team – they only had 45% of the possession. Their capacity to turn defence at one end swiftly into menace at the other is a trademark.

Hughton said: "They can do that with what they've got and the pace of Vardy. I thought we coped with that quite well.

"It's a good way of playing if you can counter-attack away from home but not everybody does it.

"More importantly, you have got to be a team that stick in there, which ever way. Whether that's great hold up play or stretching teams."

Albion managed to stay in touch until ten minutes into the second half, when Harry Maguire headed in a Mahrez corner at the far post via a slight deflection off Shane Duffy.

It was another soft goal and the ball retention, particularly in the opening 45 minutes, also fell well short of the standard required at this level to achieve results.

There will, as Hughton observed, be many more days like this. Albion will need to conjure a result from some of them to finish above the bottom three.

Albion ratings ✓

MATHEW RYAN
Won't have an easier clean sheet all season. Very little for the Australian to do behind a well-organised defence. **6**

BRUNO
Early booking left skipper treading on thin ice, although his experience would have seen him through. Replaced at half-time by Rosenior. **6**

SHANE DUFFY
Another strong, sound performance from the Republic of Ireland international. Dominant in the air inside his own area. **8**

LEWIS DUNK
Very impressive again in tandem with Duffy. Important early block from Chalobah header. Could have scored with first-half header. **8**

MARKUS SUTTNER
Early problems caused to the Austrian by Amrabat. Relief when the right-winger was subbed as a result of Britos red rejig. Did well after. **7**

ANTHONY KNOCKAERT
So close to the goal which would have delighted Albion. Started on the left but was mainly seen on the right and hit the inside of the far post. **8**

Lewis Dunk clears during a fine display at the back for Albion

DAVY PROPPER
Some good work at times in defence but still needs too long on the ball on occasion, taking momentum from attacking moves. **6**

DALE STEPHENS
Very much the midfield heartbeat of the team, doing some valuable work and sliding a couple of dangerous through passes. **7**

SOLLY MARCH
A decent supply of balls into the middle from either flank. Albion probably needed to give him more chance to run at Cathcart, then Cleverley. **7**

PASCAL GROSS
An improved performance before succumbing to cramp. Hints that he could come to life as a creator. Could there be a role other than at No.10? **6**

TOMER HEMED
His presence forced a near miss although he admitted it wasn't his final touch which sent the ball against the post. Lots of industry. **7**

SUBS
LIAM ROSENIOR: On at half-time and beaten by Richarlison before settling. 6
JOSE IZQUIERDO: Showed pace, enterprise and defensive diligence.
JAMIE MURPHY: A brief outing.

Off mark but a

Stalemate at Hornets may carry sting in tail

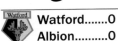

Watford	0
Albion	0

ALBION do not want their first season in the Premier League to resemble their last-but-one in the Championship, a heartbreaking catalogue of 'if only' reflections.

That is the lingering worry about a result which Chris Hughton would have bit off your hand for – and arm – before a ball had been kicked at Vicarage Road.

He ended an eventful stalemate talking about two points dropped, a rarity at this exalted level away from home, especially for a promoted team.

So many moments and matches contributed to the agonising promotion near-miss in 2015-16 before Albion made handsome amends last season.

The target has shifted now from going up to staying up. It is in this context that celebrating the first point in the Premier League has to be tempered by the inescapable conclusion it should have been the first victory.

Every point will be precious in the bid to survive and the Seagulls have entered the opening international break above the bottom three with something to build on.

That is encouraging, as was the performance, but there will not be many realistic opportunities to win away from the Amex.

The chance presented itself when Watford had Miguel Britos sent-off for a hideous challenge on Anthony Knockaert with three-quarters of the match remaining.

The Uruguayan's awful studs-up jump, which caught Knockaert on the knee and above the shin, left referee Graham Scott no choice other than to issue a red card and the Frenchman relieved that his first league start of the season after ankle ligament damage was not rudely abbreviated.

Britos has previous. Sent-off on his debut for Watford against Preston for elbowing, he was dismissed twice more last season.

Marco Silva switched Britos from the centre of defence to left-back to mark Knockaert after Jose Holebas saw red in the midweek Carabao Cup defeat by Bristol City.

Silva must have wished he had opted for youngster Brandon Mason. The experienced Britos let him down badly.

Knockaert's infectious urgency had the desired effect on Albion as an attacking threat. They were much more menacing than against

Anthony Knockaert appeals for a penalty
Pictures: Simon Dack

The moment Anthony Knockaert is cut down by Miguel Britos

Tomer Hemed goes for goal

Albion striker Tomer Hemed sees the ball come back off a post

By ANDY NAYLOR
Chief sports reporter

Manchester City or Leicester, even before the exit of Britos.

Knockaert was booed throughout by Watford fans with long memories of a dive to earn a last-gasp penalty for Leicester in a dramatic play-off semi-final four years ago.

His penalty was saved and Troy Deeney scored at the other end a few seconds later to knock Leicester out.

The effervescent winger was unlucky not to ram the insults back down the throats of the home supporters. He curled a delightful effort against the far post early on, with the grateful Heurelho Gomes well beaten.

Knockaert should have been awarded a penalty in the second half for a high foot by Abdoulaye Doucoure that caught him on the nose. Scott deemed there was no contact and gave a indirect free-kick inside the box.

Knockaert also had an angled drive tipped behind at full-stretch before giving way to record buy Jose Izquierdo as Hughton tried to induce a breakthrough.

Hughton was hampered by a bench devoid of an out-and-out striker, with Glenn Murray side-

win evades Seagulls

Watford's Andre Carillo and Albion's Davy Propper battle for the ball

the teams

Albion (4-4-1-1): Ryan; Bruno, Duffy, Dunk, Suttner; Knockaert, Stephens, Propper, March; Gross; Hemed.

Subs: Rosenior for Bruno (46), Izquierdo for Knockaert (80), Murphy for Gross (90), Maenpaa, Huenemeier, Skalak, Sidwell.

Goals: None.

Red cards: None.

Yellow card: Bruno (17) foul.

Watford (4-2-3-1): Gomes; Femenia, Prodl, Kabasele, Britos; Chalobah, Doucoure; Amrabat, Cleverley, Richarlison; Gray.

Subs: Cathcart for Amrabat (28), Carrillo for Cathcart (48), Deeney for Gray (83), Pantilimon, Success, Watson, Capoue.

Goals: None.

Red cards: Britos (24) serious foul play.

Yellow cards: None.

Referee: Graham Scott.

Attendance: 20,181.

match stats

ALBION		WATFORD
2	Shots on	0
14	Shots off	8
11	Corners	3
2	Offsides	0
18	Free-kicks conceded	7
58	Possession	42

Shane Duffy clears

ref watch

Graham Scott might have given Albion a penalty, possibly even two. But he was spot-on with the red card and when Watford appealed for Bruno to be shown a second yellow. **6**

next match

Albion v West Brom, Premier League, Saturday September 9

and table

Premier League

	P	W	D	L	F	A	Pts
Man Utd	3	3	0	0	10	0	9
Liverpool	3	2	1	0	8	3	7
Huddersfield	3	2	1	0	4	0	7
Man City	3	2	1	0	5	2	7
West Brom	3	2	1	0	3	1	7
Chelsea	3	2	0	1	6	4	6
Watford	3	1	2	0	5	3	5
Southampton	3	1	2	0	3	2	5
Tottenham	3	1	1	1	4	3	4
Burnley	3	1	1	1	4	4	4
Stoke	3	1	1	1	2	2	4
Everton	3	1	1	1	2	3	4
Swansea	3	1	1	1	2	4	4
Newcastle	3	1	0	2	3	3	3
Leicester	3	1	0	2	5	6	3
Arsenal	3	1	0	2	4	8	3
ALBION	3	0	1	2	0	4	1
Bournemouth	3	0	0	3	1	5	0
Crystal Palace	3	0	0	3	0	6	0
West Ham	3	0	0	3	2	10	0

lined by the double ankle knock he sustained at Leicester.

Tomer Hemed, probably playing his last match for the club amid strong transfer interest from the Championship, worked hard and hit the same post as Knockaert in the first half from a Solly March cross.

The circumstances of the match brutally exposed the forward shortage, which Albion will attempt to address with two signings before the window closes on Thursday evening.

They have been unfortunate so far, having lost out to Swansea for Tammy Abraham much earlier in the window and pulled the plug on Raphael Dwamena's £10 million move from FC Zurich on Friday when the Ghana international failed his medical due to a heart condition.

Sam Baldock has been sidelined as well by summer calf surgery. A pool of four strikers with different attributes is imperative in the Premier League.

Lewis Dunk and Shane Duffy were colossal again at the heart of the back four but, as Middlesbrough discovered last season, a sound defence is not enough to finish outside the relegation zone.

Izquierdo was bright in his late cameo, fizzing a shot just wide of the upright and displaying the defensive discipline Hughton demands of his wingers by chasing back to tackle and halt a rare Watford raid.

The most disappointing aspect of a third blank sheet was not troubling Gomes enough in the second half, when Watford had their number ten Tom Cleverley at right-back in a makeshift defence.

Albion were also guilty of conceding too many cheap free-kicks after the break, offering Watford a set-piece route to what would have been an improbable victory.

They are the 12th side to fail to score in their first three Premier League games. The other 11 avoided relegation. The business done between now and Thursday night will have a major bearing on whether that sequence continues.

Albion ratings ✓

MATY RYAN
Not hugely troubled but pushed over a Barry drive and stood strong to block from Morrison very late on. Confident and composed.

 7

BRUNO
The top flight suits him. Turned in another quality performance with and without the ball for two-thirds of the game. Back issue is a bit of a worry.

 7

SHANE DUFFY
West Brom had a decent spell in the middle of the first half and that was when he was at his best Was a set-piece threat.

 8

LEWIS DUNK
Centre-back has been so consistent this season and this was another strong display. Prepared to bring the ball forward when possible.

 8

MARKUS SUTTNER
Easing his way into Premier League life and this was his steadiest display yet. Was given good support by March when needed.

 7

ANTHONY KNOCKAERT
The first half impetus was more often than not involved the effervescent Frenchman. Less evident as the game wore on.

 7

Albion's No.10 Pascal Gross picked up a '9' in our ratings

DALE STEPHENS
Strong all-round display with and without the ball. Good to see him have a first-half shot, because he is capable of scoring more goals.

7

DAVY PROPPER
Encouraging signs the Dutchman is settling in after the confidence boost of two goals for his country. Forging an understanding with Stephens.

7

SOLLY MARCH
Did not always make the most of first-half crossing chances, but created the breakthrough goal and terrific defensively tracking back.

7

PASCAL GROSS
Place in club history assured as scorer of the first Premier League goal. Took both goals well and his cross for Hemed capped top contribution.

 9

TOMER HEMED
Israeli's attitude is exemplary after an unsettling transfer window. Excellent centre-forward link play for Gross's second and deserved his goal.

 8

SUBS
LIAM ROSENIOR: Slotted in for the injured Bruno.

GLENN MURRAY: Late introduction as West Brom pressed.

Victory with a

Manner of win a real tonic for fight ahead

 Albion......... 3
 West Brom .1

THE biggest positive of so many to take from Albion's first victory in the Premier League is the manner in which it was achieved.

It is difficult enough to beat any side in the care of Tony Pulis, a master of defensive organisation.

To defeat them so decisively is quite a scalp for Chris Hughton and his players.

Not as glamorous as a result against one of the top six would be, but in the context of the survival aim a real tonic.

Particularly after the disappointing end to the transfer window, when the failure to land a striker on the back of a tough opening three games without a win or a goal raised early concerns about the prospects of steering clear of the bottom three.

Hughton said: "I can understand it, because we did try and it was a position we wanted to bring in. From the supporters' point of view they did as well, but once you get to the end of the window it's the signal to work as hard as you can with the squad you've got.

"Once the window closes, as a manager you speak to the group as a whole about expectations and about 'this is it', the group of lads that have the responsibility to make sure we are in this division next season.

"Then you look for responses from them, from players that might have felt they wouldn't get as many games and it might not happen for them.

"That's how you work. Always the most important players are the ones that are here."

The last signing of the summer was supposed to be a forward, who in all probability would have replaced Tomer Hemed. The first was significant for the tactical adjustment made by Hughton to help cope with the step up.

Pascal Gross arrived from relegated Ingolstadt to fill the number ten role, playing behind one central striker rather than the twin strike force in a 4-4-2 that was fundamental to promotion.

For the system to work, he needs to exploit pockets of space between the opposition defence and midfield, and link effectively with the more advanced front man.

Gross not only scored either side of half-time, the king of assists for the past two seasons in the Bundesliga also supplied the third for

Pascal Gross rifles home the second goal for Albion against West Brom at the Amex
Pictures: Liz Finlayson

Pascal Gross, right, scores Albion's first Premier League to set the hosts on their way to victory

By ANDY NAYLOR
Chief sports reporter

Hemed. The Israeli target man was repaid for setting up Gross's second goal. Hughton could not have wished for more.

"It was ideal," he said. "I'm really pleased for both of them. They both worked hard. Tomer had almost an identical chance at Watford that hit the post. I was really pleased to see that go in."

Hemed's attitude during his time with Albion has always been exemplary. Others in his position – no new contract offer and nearly sold back to the Championship – might have been demotivated.

"Tomer came back in really good shape in the summer," Hughton said. "It's not a secret, the players generally know as much as we do.

"The strikers would have all known we were trying to bring in a striker, but that's the game. If anything it should always inspire them to do as well as they can.

"That's always the best way. It's a little bit like being dropped from the team. Once you go back in there you've got to do well enough to make sure you stay there."

Gross faces competition for the

swagger in the bag

Albion keeper Maty Ryan leaps on his team-mates as Pascal Gross celebrates his second goal

the teams

Albion (4-4-1-1): Ryan; Bruno, Duffy, Dunk, Suttner; Knockaert, Propper, Stephens, March; Gross; Hemed.

Subs: Rosenior for Bruno (62), Murray for Hemed (82), Maenpaa, Huenemeier, Skalak, Murphy, Izquierdo.

Goals: Gross (45) and (48), Hemed (64).

Red cards: None.

Yellow cards: March (89) diving, Murray (90) foul.

West Brom (4-1-4-1): Foster; Dawson, Evans, Hegazy, Nyom; Krychowiak; Phillips, Livermore, Barry, Rodriguez; Rondon.

Subs: Gibbs for Hegazi (57), Burke for Rondon (57), Morrison for Livermore (71), Yacob, Brunt, McClean, Myhill.

Goals: Morrison (78).

Red cards: None.

Yellow cards: None.

Referee: Chris Kavanagh.

Attendance: 30,381.

match stats

ALBION		WEST BROM
6	Shots on target	3
6	Shots off	9
2	Corners	6
1	Offsides	1
9	Free-kicks conceded	4
9	Possession	4

ref watch

Chris Kavanagh made his most contentious decision when booking March for diving. The Lancs official did well in only his second Premier outing and was well advised to rule out the Duffy goal for offside. **7**

next match

Bournemouth v Albion, Premier League, Friday (8pm).

and table

Premier League

	P	W	D	L	F	A	Pts
Man Utd	4	3	1	0	12	2	10
Man City	4	3	1	0	10	2	10
Chelsea	4	3	0	1	8	5	9
Watford	4	2	2	0	7	3	8
Tottenham	4	2	1	1	7	3	7
Huddersfield	3	2	1	0	4	0	7
Burnley	4	2	1	1	5	4	7
Liverpool	4	2	1	1	8	8	7
West Brom	4	2	1	1	4	4	7
Newcastle	4	2	0	2	4	3	6
Arsenal	4	2	0	2	7	8	6
Stoke	4	1	2	1	4	4	5
Southampton	4	1	2	1	3	4	5
ALBION	4	1	1	2	3	5	4
Swansea	4	1	1	2	2	5	4
Everton	4	1	1	2	2	6	4
Leicester	4	1	0	3	6	8	3
Bournemouth	4	0	0	4	1	8	0
Crystal Palace	4	0	0	4	0	7	0
West Ham	3	0	0	3	2	10	0

No.10 role, primarily from Chelsea loanee Izzy Brown. He is due to resume training tomorrow for the first time since hurting a hamstring against Manchester City on the opening day.

Gross's determination to make an impact prompted him to initially drop deep into his own territory. Hughton scowled and ushered him forward.

"I know why, because he wants to get a touch of the ball," Hughton said. "But for us and the way we want to play with Dale (Stephens) and Davy Propper, who is settling in really well, we've got two central midfield players that are good on the ball and can find bodies and space.

"I'd rather have him receiving the ball higher up the pitch than that deep."

Gross eventually damaged West Brom where Hughton wanted him, in the final third. Delivering a cross-field pass to Solly March, then re-ceiving a cross in return beyond the far post, he cut inside to score with a shot which deflected past Ben Foster via Jonny Evans.

Foster had a poor day. His handling was suspect and he thumped the ground in frustration as Gross, released by Hemed, beat him again with an angled low drive from 20 yards.

Foster's misery was complete when Hemed's header from Gross's cross squeezed past him at his near post. West Brom finally roused themselves once Pulis made changes. Substitute James Morrison pulled a goal back and anxiety increased as they threatened another, but it was far too little too late to affect the outcome.

The only other side to have scored three against them in the Premier League since March are Manchester City, a clear indication that Albion are growing into the challenge confronting them.

Kewell and Nolan to renew their old rivalry

By JAN-MALTE WAGENER
Crawley Town reporter
sport@theargus.co.uk

HARRY KEWELL is looking forward to locking horns with former rival Kevin Nolan when Crawley host high-flying Notts County today.

Former Liverpool star Kewell and ex-Bolton midfielder Nolan, pictured, met as players in the top-flight but not since 2006.

And both have stepped into management and are trying to earn their spurs as rookie bosses in League Two.

Nolan, 35, took over at the Magpies this year and his side are second in the table after three consecutive league wins while Kewell's Reds have taken four points from the last three games.

It will be the first showdown between the two as managers and Kewell is relishing squaring up to the midfielder from the other dugout.

Kewell told The Argus: "It will be nice to play against him. In former times we were tackling each other and probably now we will be arguing with each other.

"During the 90 minutes we will be enemies and afterwards we will say hello and have a chat.

"But we are both here to take the three points. We know what is at stake and we both know what needs to be done to take those three points.

"We can identify with each other's situation and this is why I think this is going to be a good game."

He added: "They are on a good run at the moment. Kevin has his team working and they've got experience at the back and up front.

"He will be a little bit edgy because he knows what I can bring, but I know what he can bring.

"I think it's going to be an aggressive game but it's going to be tactical as well. We are not afraid of the challenge."

Defender Josh Lelan, 22, is not afraid of playing a side ranked 16 places above them in the table either.

He said: "We seem to do well against teams that are doing well themselves so there is no reason not to go into it with full confidence. I'm sure we can produce a surprise but it won't be a surprise for us."

Reds are likely to make changes from the side which drew 1-1 at Stevenage on Tuesday.

Dennon Lewis is doubtful as he suffered concussion while recent signing Josh Doherty is not match fit.

Kewell said: "Dennon has done excellent throughout the whole campaign so far and finally got his start. Unfortunately he's taken a blow to the head and with the new rules of concussion you've got to be careful."

Thomas Verheydt is having medical treatment in the Netherlands and could be out for a month.

Jordan Roberts and defender Mark Connolly are also in contention.

On loan striker Ibrahim Meite scored on his debut on Tuesday.

Kewell said: "The one thing I asked Ibrahim before the last game was, 'Do you know what makes you play the next week?' He said, 'working hard' but I said 'No, goals!'."

Seagulls picked

March nets but winger Ibe turns the tide

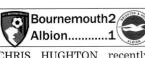

Bournemouth 2
Albion............1

CHRIS HUGHTON recently highlighted the importance in the Premier League of being able to change a game from the bench.

The assessment came back to haunt the Albion manager as opposite number Eddie Howe made a substitution in the second half which turned the prospect of a fifth successive defeat into a first win of the season for a relieved Bournemouth.

A rare header from Solly March in the 55th minute seemed set to earn the Seagulls a second successive victory and stretch their unbeaten sequence to three games.

They had frustrated the hosts, with stand-in skipper Lewis Dunk and Dale Stephens outstanding, until Howe introduced Jordan Ibe.

The talented former Liverpool winger provided clever assists for Andrew Surman in the 67th minute and six minutes later for Jermain Defoe, who pinched the points in typically clinical fashion to end his and his team's early season famine.

They are now within one point of Albion, when the gap appeared destined to be seven, Ibe's pivotal cameo a harsh reminder of how easily games can slip away at the highest level.

Hughton was forced into a change to the team which convincingly gave Albion their first Premier League win against West Brom.

Bruno, forced off in the second half by a back problem, was expected to be fit, but the Spanish veteran ended up instead as a spectator.

Hughton had in Liam Rosenior a ready-made, experienced replacement at right-back, his first league start since April 1, and Dunk captained the side.

Howe made three alterations to the team that suffered a fourth successive defeat at Arsenal.

Ex-Seagull Steve Cook was a rare absentee from the heart of the defence due to a knee injury.

Simon Francis took over, while Andrew Surman and Marc Pugh also came into the line-up for Tyrone Mings and Dan Gosling.

Bournemouth tried to impose themselves early on, but Albion threatened first, building up patiently from the back to eventually release Anthony Knockaert for a shot from 25 yards which went narrowly wide, although Asmir Begovic had it covered.

Dunk, now wearing the armband, continued his impressive start to the season in and out of possession. He pinged a couple of trademark diagonal passes which

Solly March celebrates his first Premier League goal last night at Bournemouth

Jermain Defoe rifles home the winner, centre, and is mobbed by his Bournemouth team-mates, above

By ANDY NAYLOR
Chief sports reporter

picked out Rosenior and Knockaert.

He also rescued partner Shane Duffy when the Irishman's attempted square pass to him was intercepted by Josh King.

Duffy used to play with King at Blackburn. Such generosity for a former colleague was negated by Dunk blocking the resulting attempt from the Bournemouth striker.

Albion, with Knockaert and March working hard down both flanks to help out the full-backs, kept Bournemouth at arm's length.

The hosts eventually manufactured room for the recalled Pugh to fire over from 15 yards, a rare incursion into the penalty area.

Dale Stephens, on more than one occasion, interrupted Bournemouth's progress into Albion territory with tenacious interceptions.

Charlie Daniels, spectacular scorer of Bournemouth's only goal in their opening four games against Manchester City, drove comfortably into the arms of Mathew Ryan from distance, which epitomised how difficult they were finding it to break the Seagulls down.

Albion tried to pounce on the counter-attack when the opportunity arose.

It did for Davy Propper when Harry Arter gifted the ball to him. The Dutchman, on target twice

off by the Cherries

Solly March heads home from Pascal Gross' cross to put Albion ahead against Bournemouth in their Premier League clash.
Pictures: Simon Dack

recently for his country, made progress before chipping just over the bar.

There was little evidence up to that point of Defoe ending his early drought, although he needs no invitation to pull the trigger given half a chance.

An effort on the turn from the diminutive marksman from inside the box, which flashed wide of Ryan's left-hand post, was one of the Cherries' better moments in striving to extinguish the stalemate. Albion were pressed further back in the closing stages of the first half, but they retained their discipline and composure, Bournemouth attacks relentlessly floundering around the edge of the box.

The Seagulls went close twice to taking the lead from their first corners of the contest at the start of the second half, delivered by Pascal Gross to Duffy beyond the far post.

His header and Propper's follow-up were both nodded off the line by Surman.

Duffy won the aerial battle again from the corner that followed and Stephens flicked a header against the underside of the bar from close range.

The double let-off was shortlived for Bournemouth. March, not noted for his aerial ability steered in a header from Gross's pinpoint right-wing cross to put Albion in front in the 55th minute.

Hughton's game plan had worked perfectly at that stage, but the introduction of Ibe in place of Ryan Fraser by Howe sparked a turnaround.

Ibe made an instant impact, his clever back-heel when Surman exchanged passes with him enabling the midfielder to slot Bournemouth level midway through the second half.

Six minutes later they were ahead following a corner arising from Ibe's shot from a misplaced Duffy clearance, which the outstanding Dunk diverted over the bar. Ibe was there again, dancing away on the edge of the box from Knockaert and Tomer Hemed and toepoking Defoe through for a clinical, angled finish.

Hughton threw on Glenn Murray against his old club and record buy Jose Izquierdo in what had suddenly become a retrieval mission, but the damage had been done by Ibe.

Albion ratings ✓

MATHEW RYAN
Important early save from Merino's volley, with Krul on the bench to push him as well as Maenpaa. Handling sound, kicking not the best. **7/10**

BRUNO
Good to have the skipper back. Caught upfield a couple of times when Newcastle countered first half. Vital header in frenzied finish. **7/10**

SHANE DUFFY
Customarily strong in the air. Took a yellow card for a block on Perez when he was menacing through the middle during Newcastle's late rally. **7/10**

LEWIS DUNK
Had to look twice to accept it was his mistake for Joselu's first half chance. Exceptional again otherwise, including late block of Shelvey shot. **8/10**

MARKUS SUTTNER
Austrian is proving to be a reliable acquisition after shaky game at Leicester. Snuffed out Ritchie, Newcastle's supposed danger man. **8/10**

ANTHONY KNOCKAERT
Influential first half cocktail included counter-raiding, a cross-shot for a throw and a booking. Not happy to be subbed late-on. **7/10**

Solly March in full flight

DALE STEPHENS
Had the confidence to demand the ball in tight areas in his own half. One or two passes went astray, but clever assist for the all-important goal. **8/10**

DAVY PROPPER
The Dutchman, like the team, is growing into the Premier League. Understanding with Stephens increases by the game. **7/10**

SOLLY MARCH
Performing at a consistently good level so far. Eliot denied him a second goal in as many games. Tested Yedlin at times. **7/10**

PASCAL GROSS
A pre-assist for the German this time after scoring two and creating two previously. Set piece prowess illustrated by the goal. **7/10**

TOMER HEMED
Fine finish for his second goal in as many home games. Did well again on his own through the middle, in the air and on the floor. **9/10**

SUBS
JAMIE MURPHY: Fresh pair of legs in place of Knockaert in Newcastle's late push for parity.

This win could

Hemed on target and Albion see it through

ALBION 1
NEWCASTLE 0

THERE are '13 golden games' for Albion if they are going to survive in the Premier League.

They are at the Amex against the teams other than the big six and they have now won the first two of them.

Most of their points are likely to come from these matches. Victories are precious and, after beating West Brom, they deservedly denied Newcastle a fourth on the trot.

Rafa Benitez bleated afterwards about a block by Bruno on Chancel Mbemba from the free-kick for Tomer Hemed's decisive strike.

Much was also made of an alleged stamp of retribution by Hemed on DeAndre Yedlin in response to an earlier challenge by the American international.

That may yet become retrospectively costly for Albion, with Hemed their only fit striker in the absence of the ankle-hampered Glenn Murray.

It all rather smacked of deflecting blame for a poor performance by the visitors, summed up after the final whistle by a Newcastle devotee.

Alan Shearer tweeted: "Not good enough, the better team won."

He was right. Albion were the better side for an hour, then with limited alarms held onto the lead provided by Hemed's second home goal in as many games once Benitez turned to Jonjo Shelvey and Dwight Gayle to rescue Newcastle from the bench.

Anthony Knockaert, ruled out for a month in pre-season by an ankle injury, is gradually getting his spark back.

Although the Frenchman's influence waned as the match wore on and he was unhappy to be substituted, he was the architect of several breaks which had the Newcastle defence stretched in the first quarter of the contest.

The visitors tried to sign Knockaert two summers ago and were wary of him. Every time he was on the ball it sucked in two or three players.

Knockaert inadvertently became a vital defender for Newcastle in a move he started and which Pascal Gross threatened to end.

The German's swivelling shot from eight yards was goalbound when it struck his team-mate.

There were encouraging signs in possession that Albion are growing into the Premier League game by game. They were on the

Albion enjoy their win while Newcastle's Jonjo Shelvey shows his dejection

Tomer Hemed starts the celebrations

So unlucky as Knockaert blocks Gross shot

By Andy Naylor
Chief sports reporter

front foot and the more fluent team in the first half, but the striker shortage remains a huge handicap for Chris Hughton.

Hemed found himself isolated at times. On one occasion No.10 Gross was at right-back when he cleared up to the outnumbered Israeli on halfway.

Newcastle, with less possession, had chances in the opening 45 minutes to gain a flattering foothold.

Spanish midfielder Mikel Merino, on loan from Borussia Dortmund, looks an accomplished addition. His early volley from a corner forced Mathew Ryan into a one-handed stop.

It was a big moment for the Australian, with Tim Krul on the bench to press him following the Dutchman's move from Newcastle.

Merino's fellow countryman Joselu should have scored when he turned and shot from a rare error by Lewis Dunk.

The source was Christian Atsu down the left flank. It was a problem area for Albion a couple of times when Bruno, returning from a back injury, was caught upfield

be so very precious

Tomer Hemed hooks home the winner to give Albion three precious points against Newcastle. Picture by Liz Finlayson

after attacks broke down.

A sharper finisher would have punished them. Joselu let his old club Stoke off the hook three times in Newcastle's previous game.

They almost led against the run of play at the interval, but Ayoze Perez shot over when Mbemba popped up in the box from left-back to feed him.

The pre-match focus was on the danger from Newcastle from set plays via Matt Ritchie and the head of captain Jamaal Lascelles, which was responsible for their wins against Swansea and Stoke.

So it was satisfying for Albion to catch them napping and seize the advantage six minutes after the break with a routine straight from the training ground.

Gross's free-kick was drilled to the far post, where Dale Stephens had peeled away to be totally unmarked. His header down and back across the face of the box was hooked into the roof of the net by Hemed in instinctive fashion.

Albion had Newcastle rocking for a period after the goal. Solly March nearly doubled the lead from an acute angle from Bruno's cross. The outstretched right boot of keeper Rob Elliot kept the visitors in contention.

Shelvey, unable to force his way back into the starting line-up since a red card on the opening day, and last season's top scorer Gayle induced a quest for parity.

Shelvey took over set piece duties from the disappointing Ritchie. He hit the near post from a corner, which the scrambling Ryan had covered.

Although Newcastle pushed hard for an equaliser in the closing stages, that and a shot on the turn by Gayle saved by Ryan were the closest they came.

Albion resisted with relative comfort. Their first clean sheet at home was hard-earned and warranted.

Newcastle edged them out in the Championship last season, but they have only two points in hand of them now.

the teams

Albion (4-4-1-1): Ryan; Bruno, Duffy, Dunk, Suttner; Knockaert, Propper, Stephens, March; Gross; Hemed.
Subs: Murphy for Knockaert (81), Krul, Huenemeier, Izquierdo, Schelotto, Rosenior, Brown.
Goals: Hemed (51).
Red cards: None.
Yellow cards: Knockaert (13) foul, Duffy (76) foul.

Newcastle (4-2-3-1): Elliot; Yedlin, Lascelles, Clark, Mbemba; Hayden, Merino; Ritchie, Perez, Atsu; Joselu.
Subs: Shelvey for Hayden (68), Gayle for Josleu (71), Gemz for Memba (83), Darlow, J. Murphy, Diame, Manquillo.
Goals: None.
Red cards: None.
Yellow cards: Lascelles (90) foul.

stats

ALBION		NEWCASTLE
3	On target	5
4	Off target	12
2	Corners	8
1	Offsides	1
6	Free-kicks against	8

ref watch

There was some debate about a stamp but Andre Marriner had a sound game - and Anthony Knockaert gave him one of his easier yellow card decisons early on! 7

next up

Arsenal v Albion, Premier League, Sunday, 12 noon.

and table

Premier League

	P	W	D	L	F	A	Pts
Man City	6	5	1	0	21	2	16
Man Utd	6	5	1	0	17	2	16
Chelsea	6	4	1	1	12	5	13
Tottenham	6	3	2	1	10	5	11
Liverpool	6	3	2	1	12	11	11
Watford	6	3	2	1	9	10	11
Huddersfield	6	2	3	1	5	3	9
Burnley	6	2	3	1	6	5	9
Newcastle	6	3	0	3	6	5	9
West Brom	5	2	2	1	4	4	8
Southampton	6	2	2	2	4	5	8
Arsenal	5	2	1	2	7	8	7
ALBION	6	2	1	3	5	7	7
Everton	6	2	1	3	4	11	7
Swansea	6	1	2	3	5	7	5
Stoke	6	1	2	3	5	10	5
Leicester	6	1	1	4	9	12	4
West Ham	6	1	1	4	6	13	4
Bournemouth	6	1	0	5	4	11	0
West Ham	1	0	0	1	0	4	0

Albion ratings ✓

MATHEW RYAN
Continued his good form since the first couple of games. Save from Ramsey with his feet the best of several in the first half.
 8

BRUNO
Bit harsh to face such strong opposition away on 37th birthday. Pretty sound defensively. Few opportunities to venture forward.
 7

SHANE DUFFY
So powerful in the air. Not quite as dependable on the floor. One loose clearance could have been costly and second booking in two games.
7

LEWIS DUNK
Apart from giving the ball away once in dangerous area in the first half, he was excellent again. Confidently came forward to shoot once.
 8

GAETAN BONG
Handed first start of the season ahead of Suttner and did okay. Couple of stray passes, but linked well with Izquierdo in the first half.
 7

DALE STEPHENS
Grew into the game after that initial period when Albion could barely get on the ball.
 6

Gaetan Bong was preferred ahead of Markus Suttner at full-back

DAVY PROPPER
Looked to be the man charged with giving Brown help if possible. Worked hard out of possession but needed to test Cech with two chances.
6

PASCAL GROSS
A deeper position and almost paid dearly for a loose first-half pass. Could not be as influential as he has been of late.
6

JOSE IZQUIERDO
A tough first Premier start against an Arsenal side who looked to use Bellerin's threat. Gave away a costly free-kick but later teed up Propper.
5

SOLLY MARCH
Continues to show massive promise and confidence at this level. Hit the post, cleared off the line and perhaps deserved better service.
7

IZZY BROWN
A tough ask as he battled away on his own out of position. Was a handful on occasions and glanced a header wide.
 6

SUBS
Ezequiel Schelotto: Keen to get forward.
Anthony Knockaert: Looked fired up, hungry and lively on the left.
Glenn Murray: Close to reducing arrears when he got in front of Mustafi.

Albion holding

Defeat but Seagulls look like they belong

 Arsenal........2
 Albion..........0

SO FAR so good. Albion are holding their own in the Premier League, on course for survival with a point a game.

And as Chris Hughton pointed out after a predictably routine defeat at Arsenal, it could have been better but for the points dropped at Bournemouth in particular and also at Watford.

They continued to be competitive and to look as if they belong at this level, once they had recovered from a step back in their progression in the early stages at the Emirates.

They were so deep that even Izzy Brown, operating as an emergency number nine due to the injury and suspension crisis up front, was only 30 yards from his own goal.

Lesser sides would have capitulated after conceding early, but Albion grew into the game without ever threatening to cause an upset once Arsenal doubled their lead early in the second half.

Hughton would have feared, when the fixtures were released, the potential for hammerings in the opening seven matches, first up at home to Manchester City and then Arsenal, and the accompanying damage to confidence for a club and players finding their feet among the elite.

That has not happened and, in contrast to other more established Premier League outfits, Albion look solid enough to suggest it will not occur often, if at all, from here on either.

Consider what Manchester City and Arsenal have done to opponents apart from their 2-0 wins over Hughton's newcomers.

City scored four or more against Liverpool, Watford, Crystal Palace and Feyenoord. Leicester, Bournemouth and Cologne all conceded three or more at the Emirates.

Huddersfield had a go early on against Spurs – and found themselves three down. Talk of their wise early recruitment has soon evaporated.

The danger of a drubbing by over-committing becomes greater as the quality of the opposition increases.

Late in the first half, Albion had a corner. Solly March was crowded out, Arsenal swarmed forward rapidly in numbers and only a fine save by Mathew Ryan with his shins from Aaron Ramsey stopped them taking a 2-0 lead into the break.

Hughton's selection, in the cir-

By ANDY NAYLOR
Chief sports reporter

cumstances, was as bold as he could afford to be.

He went for pace and athleticism in the hope of stretching Arsenal when the opportunity arose with March, Brown and Jose Izquierdo,

given his first start at the expense of Anthony Knockaert.

It was sensible adventure, Pascal Gross dropping back into midfield and Gaetan Bong offering more defensive security at left-back.

It will get easier than this for record signing Izquierdo. The Colombian gave away the free-kick from which Arsenal opened the scoring and generally struggled, apart from one or two attacking flashes in the first half.

Albion protested the ball had gone out beyond the far post when the free-kick was headed back for Nacho Monreal to ram in his first league goal since March 2013 after Shkodran Mustafi's shot had been blocked.

That was 16 minutes in and French marksman Alexandre Lacazette had already lashed against a post by then from outside the box in his quest to become the first Arsenal player to score in his

Striker Glenn Murray heads narrowly wide for Albion in the closing moments. Pictures: Simon Dack

Alex Iwobi powers his strike past Mathew Ryan after being set free by Alexis Sanchez's back-heel

Albion players look dejected after Alex Iwobi had scored Arsenal's second goal at the Emirates

their own in Prem

Centre-half Shane Duffy shows his frustration

the teams

Albion (4-3-3): Ryan; Bruno, Duffy, Dunk, Bong; Stephens, Gross, Propper; March, Brown, Izquierdo.

Subs: Schelotto for March (70), Knockaert for Izquierdo (76), Murray for Brown (76), Krul, Goldson, Suttner, Molumby.

Goals: None.

Red cards: None.

Yellow cards: Gross (17) dissent, Duffy (39) foul.

Arsenal (3-4-2-1): Cech; Holding, Mustafi, Monreal; Bellerin, Ramsey, Xhaka, Kolasinac; Iwobi, Sanchez; Lacazette.

Subs: Giroud for Lacazette (70), Walcott for Iwobi (70), Elneny for Xhaka (83), Mertesacker, Wilshere, Ospina, Maitland-Niles.

Goals: Monreal (16), Iwobi (56)..

Red cards: None.

Yellow cards: None.

Referee: Kevin Friend.

Attendance: 59,378.

stats

ALBION		ARSENAL
1	Shots on	11
8	Shots off	14
5	Corners	6
0	Offsides	1
8	free-kicks	7
35	possession	65

referee

Kevin Friend looked he got the big calls right and was correctly advised on the first goal, despite Albion complaints. **8**

next up

Albion v Everton, Sunday October 15 (1.30pm).

and table

Premier League

	P	W	D	L	F	A	Pts
Man City	7	6	1	0	22	2	19
Man Utd	7	6	1	0	21	2	19
Tottenham	7	4	2	1	14	5	14
Chelsea	7	4	1	2	12	6	13
Arsenal	7	4	1	2	11	8	13
Burnley	7	3	3	1	7	5	12
Liverpool	7	3	3	1	13	12	12
Watford	7	3	3	1	11	12	12
Newcastle	7	3	1	3	7	6	10
West Brom	7	2	3	2	6	8	9
Huddersfield	7	2	3	2	5	7	9
Southampton	7	2	2	3	5	7	8
Stoke	7	2	2	3	7	11	8
ALBION	7	2	1	4	5	9	7
West Ham	7	2	1	4	7	13	7
Everton	7	2	1	4	4	12	7
Leicester	7	1	2	4	9	12	5
Swansea	7	1	2	4	3	8	5
Bournemouth	7	1	1	5	4	11	4
Crystal Palace	7	0	0	7	0	17	0

---

first four league appearances since 1958.

Falling behind, far from terrorising Albion, actually galvanised them. They nearly levelled when room was created from another of their free-kick routines for Arsenal supporter March to strike a post from 20 yards.

It was the same old Arsenal at times, a joy going forward, unconvincing at the back in spite of their sequence of four clean sheets since

Liverpool thumped them.

Alex Iwobi removed any doubt about the result early in the second half, firing past the excellent Ryan into the roof of the net from a delightful back-heel by Alexis Sanchez, a reminder of the Chilean's class on an afternoon when he sometimes appeared disinterested.

The same could be said of the Arsenal supporters, subdued by a noon kick-off and the expectation of a comfortable victory.

It was, but the Albion fans were determined to enjoy themselves and they remained in good spirits.

They nearly had a goal to cheer during a late rally when Glenn Murray, introduced in tandem with Knockaert, got across the defender at the near post to head just wide from the type of service from Gross that he thrives on.

In other instances throughout the match a bit more precision and ambition in possession from Albion

would have given Arsene Wenger, celebrating 21 years in charge, more anxiety about completing a victory against a 45th different Premier League club, surpassing for once Sir Alex Ferguson.

Albion go to Mourinho's Manchester United next month. Their Premier League future will not be decided by fixtures like that or this one, so much as those before it against Everton, West Ham, Southampton, Swansea and Stoke.

Albion ratings ✔

MATHEW RYAN
Gets better and better. It took a penalty from England's record scorer to beat him – and even then he had the final word to save a point. **8**

BRUNO
Tough to rate as he was excellent for much of the game – and inspired for the opener. But it looked like he was guilty on that penalty. **6**

LEWIS DUNK
Lots of good work again and almost scored when he claimed a shot was handled. He will face better out-and-out strikers this season. **7**

SHANE DUFFY
Was adding to his list of rock-solid performances when injury cut things short. A soaring presence in the air again. **8**

MARKUS SUTTNER
Was given problems by Vlasic and was lucky when his opponent slipped as he shot. But was also a contributor going forward **6**

ANTHONY KNOCKAERT
Recalled after he was relegated to the bench at Arsenal. Put in a good shift and his first Prem goal could lead to greater influence. **7**

Bruno applauds the fans after the final whistle on a mixed day for the Albion captain

DALE STEPHENS
Effective once more as a shield for the defence, although passing was not always up to his normal high standard. Shot over in first half. **6**

DAVY PROPPER
Fit after rested from Holland's midweek game with a hip injury, the Dutchman produced a mixed bag. **6**

SOLLY MARCH
Even battle going both ways with Holgate. Tracked back diligently. Delivery into the box could have been better after promising bursts. **6**

PASCAL GROSS
Uncharacteristically gave possession away several times early on. Determination to keep the ball alive prompted Knockaert's breakthrough. **6**

GLENN MURRAY
Tough first home start of the season, up against Keane and Jagielka. Short of peak fitness after ankle trouble and fed off scraps. **6**

SUBS

Jose Izquierdo: Lively late cameo on home debut.
Uwe Huenemeier: Solid for injured Duffy.
Izzy Brown: Tested Pickford after combining with Izquierdo.

Spot of bother

Penalty is tough on Seagulls in tight draw

 Albion..........1
 Everton........1

ALBION are entitled to feel the rub of the green is going against them so far in the Premier League.

First it was Tomer Hemed, banned for treading on Newcastle defender DeAndre Yedlin, deliberately according to an FA panel.

The Israeli striker, sitting out the second of a three-match suspension, may well have suffered a lesser punishment, or none at all, had it not been for the live coverage on Sky and ensuing fuss.

The only live coverage this time was abroad, in India and elsewhere. Instead, it was the sharp eye of referee Michael Oliver which denied Albion a third straight home win.

Oliver spotted Bruno catching Dominic Calvert-Lewin in the neck with an elbow from a free-kick. Wayne Rooney sent Mathew Ryan the wrong way to earn Everton a point wrong way to rescue Everton and, possibly, their under-pressure manager Ronald Koeman.

It could be argued justice was done. The result was about right on balance and the free-kick arose from Albion goalscorer Anthony Knockaert cynically clipping Kevin Mirallas from behind as the substitute counter-attacked.

The yellow card for the Frenchman was inevitable, the resulting punishment from Oliver and Rooney hard to take for Knockaert following his first-ever Premier League goal – and particularly tough for Bruno.

The veteran Spaniard, who was also booked, was still fuming after the final whistle. He did not appear best pleased with Knockaert sharing pleasantries with Oliver, whose decision to point to the spot highlighted the age-old frustration for managers and players of inconsistency. Physical contact and varying degrees of skulduggery are commonplace at every set-piece in the modern game. Sometimes referees see it, on many other occasions they miss it.

Bruno's angst was compounded by Oliver and his assistants rejecting a couple of penalty appeals by Albion. On another day Lewis Dunk's angled drive in the first half, which hit Michael Keane on the chest, then arm, as he blocked it, could have been given.

In the second half, Pascal Gross was convinced Leighton Baines nudged him over in an aerial duel. One camera angle suggested the German had a case, another from

Anthony Knockaert scores to put Albion ahead in their Premier League clash against Everton

Wayne Rooney converts from the spot as he sends Mathew Ryan the wrong way to earn Everton a point

Lewis Dunk leads the appeals for a penalty after his goalbound shot hits an arm in the first half

By ANDY NAYLOR
Chief sports reporter

behind the goal less so, which emphasises just how difficult it is for referees to get it right in real time.

It felt afterwards for manager Chris Hughton and his players like two points dropped, having led so late, but the disappointment should not linger for too long. The 13 games at the Amex, aside from the top six, are going to be key in the quest for survival. Hughton's side now have a healthy seven points from the first three of them against West Brom, Newcastle and Everton. This was the sternest test of that trio, in spite of what the early table suggests. Everton have too much quality in their ranks to remain in relegation trouble.

Their early control fizzled out as Albion demonstrated once more that their biggest strength is their defensive resilience.

Shane Duffy and Lewis Dunk were customarily outstanding at the heart of the back four. So too behind them was Ryan, who in company with Duffy was back from an exhausting and exhilarating week helping his country within a play-off of next summer's World Cup finals in Russia.

Duffy, a rock both for the Republic of Ireland against Wales and against his first club Everton, was

as Albion are denied

Anthony Knockaert is mobbed after scoring
Pictures: Liz Finlayson and Simon Dack

the teams

Albion (4-4-1-1): Ryan; Bruno, Duffy, Dunk, Suttner; Knockaert, Stephens, Propper, March; Gross; Murray.

Subs: Izquierdo for March (74), Huenemeier for Duffy (74), Brown for Murray (84), Krul, Bong, Schelotto, Molumby.

Goal: Knockaert (82).

Red cards: None.

Yellow cards: Propper (52) foul, Dunk (67) foul, Bruno (89) foul, Knockaert (90) foul.

Everton (4-2-3-1): Pickford; Holgate, Keane, Jagielka, Baines; Gueye, Schneiderlin; Vlasic, Sigurdsson, Calvert-Lewin; Rooney.

Subs: Niasse for Gueye (69), Mirallas for Baines (82), Davies for Rooney (90), Stekelenburg, Williams, Martina, Klaassen.

Goal: Rooney (90) penalty.

Red cards: None.

Yellow cards: Mirallas (90) foul.

Referee: Michael Oliver.

Attendance: 30,565 (3,003 away).

match stats

ALBION		EVERTON
3	Shots on target	6
9	Shots off	7
7	Corners	1
12	Offsides	10
12	Free-kicks against	10
47%	Possession	53%

Emotion runs high as Anthony Knockaert is lifted to his feet

ref watch

Michael Oliver was booed off but he probably got the penalty decision right amid a confused penalty box. Arguably got a few things wrong, not all of them in Everton's favour. **6**

next game

West Ham v Albion, Premier League, Friday (8pm).

and table

Premier League

	P	W	D	L	F	A	Pts
Man City	8	7	1	0	29	4	22
Man Utd	8	6	2	0	21	2	20
Tottenham	8	5	2	1	15	5	17
Watford	8	4	3	1	13	13	15
Chelsea	8	4	1	3	13	8	13
Arsenal	8	4	1	3	12	10	13
Burnley	8	3	4	1	8	6	13
Liverpool	8	3	4	1	13	12	13
Newcastle	8	3	2	3	9	8	11
Southampton	8	2	3	3	7	9	9
West Brom	7	2	3	2	6	8	9
Huddersfield	8	2	3	3	5	9	9
Swansea	8	2	2	4	5	8	8
ALBION	8	2	2	4	6	10	8
West Ham	8	2	2	4	8	14	8
Everton	8	2	2	4	5	13	8
Stoke	8	2	2	4	9	18	8
Leicester	7	1	2	4	9	12	5
Bournemouth	8	1	1	6	4	12	4
Crystal Palace	8	1	0	7	2	18	3

forced off with 15 minutes left by a minor groin injury.

Influential as he has been, Albion need not take any risks with Duffy at this stage of the season. They have his replacement, Uwe Huenemeier, and Connor Goldson in reserve, while West Ham do not have the aerial threat of Andy Carroll on Friday after his red card at Burnley.

Ryan, meanwhile, after travelling over 30,000 miles for Australia, continued his fine run of form.

He dived to his right to keep out Idrissa Gueye's first-half shot, and again acrobatically early in the second half from an effort from closer range and struck with more ferocity by Mason Holgate.

Ryan reserved his best until last, depriving Mirallas both from his own shot and then when the ball rebounded goalwards off the Belgian via Dunk in the same incident.

Imagine how much more painful it would have been if Albion had lost and dropped to 17th rather than remaining 14th, still above Everton on goal difference.

Moving up to tenth beckoned when the increasing threat from the Seagulls as the second half wore on was rewarded. The overlapping Bruno got the better of Calvert-Lewin to set up Jose Izquierdo for a shot which Keane blocked. Morgan Schneiderlin should have completed the clearance, but he was too slow to react and Gross fed Knockaert to drill past Jordan Pickford.

Izquierdo made an impact when he came on. The Colombian signing forced Pickford into his first serious save before Knockaert's goal, then combined with Izzy Brown for his fellow sub to test Pickford again.

Albion would have been 2-0 up and home and dry. Minutes later, Oliver walked off to boos reserved previously throughout for Rooney.

That rub of the green needs rebalancing, especially as Yedlin - Hemed's 'victim' - somehow escaped a blatant second yellow card from Kevin Friend in Newcastle's subsequent draw at Southampton.

Reds' Smith apologises to the fans as Hatters visit

By MIKE LEGG
Football reporter
mike.legg@theargus.co.uk

CRAWLEY skipper Jimmy Smith has apologised to supporters and told them the players "owe them" a performance as leaders Luton Town visit today.

Former Albion player and first team coach Nathan Jones brings the in-form Hatters to the Checkatrade Stadium while Crawley are still licking their wounds after a disappointing 2-0 defeat to bottom side Chesterfield in midweek.

In an open letter to disgruntled Reds fans, Smith, pictured, said: "First of all, we owe an apology to our fans who turned up for Tuesday's game against Chesterfield.

"The performance was unacceptable

League Two

	P	W	D	L	F	A	Pts
Luton	14	9	3	2	34	12	30
Notts County	14	9	2	3	24	15	29
Exeter	14	9	2	3	22	16	29
Wycombe	14	7	5	2	28	21	26
Accrington	14	8	2	4	24	18	26
Newport Co	14	7	3	4	22	14	24
Stevenage	14	7	3	4	23	22	24
Coventry	14	7	2	5	14	8	23
Lincoln City	14	6	5	3	16	13	23
Swindon	14	7	1	6	20	18	22
Grimsby	14	6	3	5	19	21	21
Mansfield	14	5	5	4	20	19	20
Cambridge U	14	6	2	6	14	15	20
Colchester	14	5	3	6	20	20	18
Carlisle	14	5	3	6	19	20	18
Cheltenham	14	5	2	7	19	20	17
Crewe	14	5	2	7	15	20	17
Yeovil	14	4	3	7	20	28	15
Crawley Town	14	4	2	8	12	16	14
Barnet	14	3	4	7	17	19	13
Morecambe	14	3	4	7	12	20	13
Port Vale	14	3	2	9	15	20	11
Forest Green	14	2	3	9	12	31	9
Chesterfield	14	2	2	10	12	27	8

and after the game we had a long chat amongst ourselves and with the team management about how we can put things right. We totally appreciate the frustration of our fans about our home performances this season.

"Our home form has not been good enough but tomorrow would be a great game to start turning it around.

"We owe it to everyone connected with the club to produce a performance to be proud of. There is no bigger test in the league at the moment than playing the leaders Luton Town, but the game at the Checkatrade Stadium is one we are really looking forward to."

Luton are in search of a fifth consecutive win and have Reds top scorer last season James Collins as an option.

Reds boss Harry Kewell said: "They've got some of the best forward players in the division so it'll be a tough game but I would say the pressure is on them. In an odd way perhaps you could say it's a free game for us and our results at home probably don't reflect the performances on the whole."

Albion come of

West Ham hammered by rampant Seagulls

West Ham..0
Albion........3

REMEMBER the date, 20th October 2017. The day Albion came of age in the Premier League.

They have waited since 1983 for an away win in the top flight of English football.

Not any more. That statistic was emphatically erased with a gold medal display from the men in gold shirts in the stadium that staged the London 2012 Olympics.

It is home now to West Ham, who were humiliated. Glenn Murray scored twice, the second a penalty, either side of a cracking strike from record buy Jose Izquierdo to lift Albion, for a few hours at least to the giddy heights of tenth.

It was some way to reverse the trend.

Albion had scored once and taken only a point from their first four away fixtures.

Chris Hughton got his selection spot-on, starting with Izquierdo and Gaetan Bong who had a fine game behind the Colombian as part of a rock-solid defence.

Hughton made two amendments to the team held 1-1 at home by Everton.

Bong returned at left-back for Markus Suttner.

Record signing Jose Izquierdo made his second appearance in front of Bong at the expense of Solly March, scorer of Albion's only goal in their opening four away games at Bournemouth.

Shane Duffy recovered from the groin injury which forced him off towards the end of the Everton deadlock, when three points became one with a late Wayne Rooney penalty given away by Bruno.

The resurrection by Hughton of the left-sided partnership he switched to at Arsenal was based on sound logic. Bong and Izquierdo linked well at times at the Emirates.

In choosing Bong over Suttner, Hughton will also have taken into account the threat down West Ham's right from the powerful Michail Antonio.

March, Albion's most consistent attacker so far, was a little unlucky to be left out, although Hughton will be mindful of not burning him out.

It's a long battle when the aim is survival.

Hammers boss Slaven Bilic, limited up front by the absences of Andy Carroll (suspended) and Diafra Sakho (injured) could still field a potent attack of Antonio, Manuel Lanzini and Marko Arnautovic behind Javier Hernandez.

Pedro Obiang came into the midfield and Arthur Masuaku was preferred at left-back to Aaron

Glenn Murray heads Albion into a first-half lead against West Ham last night   Pictures: Simon Dack

Jose Izquierdo lets fly with his right foot after cutting in from the left to score past Joe Hart

Albion striker Glenn Murray scores from the penalty spot to secure a 3-0 victory

By ANDY NAYLOR
Chief sports reporter

Cresswell.

The atmosphere among the home supporters was jittery to begin with and it transmitted to the players.

Albion settled better and exploited poor defending to take a tenth minute lead.

The marking was awful from West Ham. Clever movement was not required by Murray, he simply guided in a header in-between defenders from Pascal Gross's pinpoint free-kick.

Murray's first Premier League goal since the winner for Bournemouth at Chelsea in December 2015 emphasised he will score with the type of service he thrives on.

Gross is capable of providing it. The German's fourth assist maintained his impressive sequence of having a hand in Albion's first seven Premier League goals.

He scored twice against West Brom and Tomer Hemed's winner against Newcastle started with his free-kick.

Albion had to weather spells of pressure for the rest of the first half, which occasionally galvanised the West Ham supporters.

Pablo Zabaleta picked out Lanzini in space beyond the far post. Bong did just enough to deflect the shot over for a corner.

Izquierdo had to do plenty of tracking back.

The fleet-footed Colombian did it well to block an Antonio cross,

age in the Premier

Glenn Murray celebrates his opening goal
Picture: Simon Dack

Jose Izquierdo is left on the ground after being mobbed

ref watch

Didn't have a huge amount to do but got the penalty right and rightly booked Hernandez for his clumsy foul on Knockaert. **7**

next up

Albion v Southampton, Premier League, Sunday Oct 29, 1.30pm

and table

Premier League

	P	W	D	L	F	A	Pts
Man City	8	7	1	0	29	4	22
Man Utd	8	6	2	0	21	2	20
Tottenham	8	5	2	1	15	5	17
Watford	8	4	3	1	13	13	15
Chelsea	8	4	1	3	13	8	13
Arsenal	8	4	1	3	12	10	13
Burnley	8	3	4	1	8	6	13
Liverpool	8	3	4	1	13	12	13
Newcastle	8	3	2	3	9	8	11
ALBION	9	3	2	4	9	10	11
West Brom	8	2	4	2	7	9	10
Southampton	8	2	3	3	7	9	9
Huddersfield	8	2	3	3	5	9	9
Swansea	8	2	2	4	5	8	8
Everton	8	2	2	4	5	13	8
Stoke	8	2	2	4	9	18	8
West Ham	9	2	2	5	8	17	8
Leicester	8	1	3	4	10	13	6
Bournemouth	8	1	1	6	4	12	4
Crystal Palace	8	1	0	7	2	18	3

---

less well when Zabaleta went by. The shot from Hernandez in the box that resulted produced a brave block by Duffy, defending with customary gusto.

Having held firm, Albion tightened their grip on the contest just before the break.

Murray, released inside the area by a combination of Gross and Dale Stephens, was denied by a fine save by Joe Hart.

The respite was brief for England's No.1 and his fal-

tering team-mates. Izquierdo cut inside onto his right-foot, as he loves to do. The shot carried too much venom for the diving Hart, who got a hand to it but could not keep it out.

The half-time whistle shortly afterwards was greeted with boos by the West Ham fans. Albion's were ecstatic.

Bilic brought on Andre Ayew for the second half to give more support to Hernandez.

Cheikhou Kouyate gave way and Lanzini dropped back into midfield.

They struggled to make much headway against Albion's solid back four.

Duffy and Lewis Dunk were strong again in the middle, Bong and Bruno contained the respective threats from Antonio and Arnautovic.

One free-kick from Lanzini, which sailed 15 yards over the bar, summed up West Ham's incompetence.

Another just after was more dangerous, brushing off Duffy in the wall for a corner with the rarely bothered Mathew Ryan diving to cover.

Izquierdo looked a little surprised - and a little tired - when March replaced him in the 69th minute.

It made sense, as Izquierdo is still not quite up to speed after a summer disrupted by his move from Brugge. Albion rubbed salt into West Ham's gaping

wounds. A dazzling run and pass from Anthony Knockaert ended with Murray denied at a tight angle by Hart.

Not for long. Zabaleta upended him at the far post and Murray calmly converted his second and Albion's third from the spot.

That was the signal for West Ham fans to leave the stadium in droves, their side humiliated by a professional and clinical away display by Albion.

Albion ratings ✓

MATHEW RYAN
No chance with the Ward-Prowse free-kick which hit the woodwork for Davis to give Saints early lead. Little for the Australian to do otherwise. **7**

BRUNO
Sound performance by the veteran Spaniard on his 200th club appearance. Boufal did not offer much against him. **7**

SHANE DUFFY
Had chances to score with first-half header over and second half shot wide. Redeemed himself for silly foul and booking with brave header. **7**

LEWIS DUNK
Ability to defend and play summarised on one hand by vital deflection on Gabbiadini shot at 1-1, on the other by fine crossfield pass to Bruno. **7**

GAETAN BONG
Solid on his first home start in the Premier League. Kept the substituted Tadic on a tight rein. Late booking for full-blooded tackle on Long. **7**

ANTHONY KNOCKAERT
One of the players who worked so hard to make things happen against Saints' organised ranks. Created a chance for Murray. **7**

Albion's Bruno made his 200th club appearance in the draw at the Amex

DAVY PROPPER
Looks high class in flashes but was not a prominent figure this time. Got a header on target from a set-piece. **7**

DALE STEPHENS
Foul ahead of the Southampton goal proved costly but did some good stuff after that and is looking more comfortable in possession. **7**

JOSE IZQUIERDO
Flitted in and out but is a bundle of energy and his pace offers of a great option. Had a goal bound shot blocked. **7**

PASCAL GROSS
Pinpoint delivery for the goal. Not so accurate on other occasions when he got into good areas but was lively and found pockets of space. **8**

GLENN MURRAY
Must be a headache to play against. Clever work for the goal and also got in a precious defensive header late on. **7**

SUBS
IZZY BROWN: Sent on near the end in the No.10 role with Albion on the back foot.
SOLLY MARCH: A brief run out down the left.

Seagulls battle

Hosts show character in response to early blow

Albion.............1
Southampton.1

OFTEN, a draw at home feels like a defeat.

It certainly did against Everton in the previous home game, when Bruno gave away a late penalty.

Not this time. Another 1-1 draw feels like a point gained in the quest to stay in the Premier League.

Chris Hughton would certainly have accepted that at half-time, with his team trailing early and Southampton looking relatively comfortable.

By the end, the visitors were grateful for parity. Albion were the likelier winners once Glenn Murray levelled early in the second half with his third goal in two games.

Just past the opening quarter of the season, Hughton's side resembles an authentic mid-table Premier League team, good enough not to be humiliated by the top six and to take points, home and away, from everybody else.

Since finishing runners-up to Albion in League One in 2010-11 and coming second again in the Championship the following year, Southampton have ended up 14th, eighth, seventh, sixth and eighth.

In spite of several managerial changes, Mauricio Pellegrino the latest, they are a well-established and well-organised Premier League outfit.

Although Albion were a little fortunate that central midfielder Mario Lemina, comfortably Southampton's best player so far this season, was missing through injury, they more than matched them.

That bodes well for the challenges ahead. Rest assured, there are many more to come.

A decent haul from the next two games either side of the international break, at Swansea on Saturday and at home to Stoke, would be helpful, with Manchester United, Liverpool and Spurs looming in the next five fixtures after that.

Every point matters in inching to the 40, or slightly fewer, that will be required to survive.

After scoring early themselves at West Ham, Albion eventually ran out comfortable winners, such was the ineptitude of the Hammers.

The Seagulls' own response to initial adversity at home was contrastingly robust, at least in the second half when they lifted the tempo and Southampton felt the heat.

One area they need to be wary

Glenn Murray heads home the equaliser for Albion against Southampton   Pictures: Liz Finlayson and Simon Dack

Anthony Knockaert lets fly for Albion against Southampton at the Amex

By ANDY NAYLOR
Chief sports reporter

of is conceding cheap free-kicks in dangerous positions. They are making a bit of an unwanted habit of that and, in the Premier League, you risk severe punishment. So it proved seven minutes in, when Dale Stephens brought down Sofiane Boufal 25 yards out.

The ensuing free-kick from James Ward-Prowse, expertly struck with elevation to clear the defensive wall and then dip, beat Mathew Ryan as it struck the upright.

Steven Davis stooped to conquer, nodding the rebound to give Southampton a platform to earn their first away win of a lopsided start to the season in which they had played twice as many matches at home as away.

Albion were back on terms seven minutes into the restart, via the combination that provided swift impetus against West Ham.

Pascal Gross crossed from the right and Glenn Murray, although having to retreat to reach it be-

back for vital point

Southampton's James Ward-Prowse gets his free-kick up and over the Albion wall in the build-up to the opening goal

the teams

Albion (4-4-1-1): Ryan; Bruno, Duffy, Dunk, Bong; Knockaert, Stephens, Propper, Izquierdo; Gross; Murray.

Subs: Brown for Gross (84), March for Izquierdo (87), Krul, Hemed, Goldson, Schelotto, Suttner.

Goals: Murray (52).

Red cards: None.

Yellow cards: Murray (62) foul, Duffy (80) kicking ball away, Bong (90) foul.

Southampton (4-1-2-3): Forster; Cedric, Hoedt, Van Dijk, Bertrand; Romeu; Ward-Prowse, Davis; Tadic, Gabbiadini, Boufal.

Subs: Redmond for Boufal (72), Long for Tadic (84), Hojbjerg for Ward-Prowse (84), McCarthy, Yoshida, J. Stephens, McQueen.

Goals: Davis (7).

Red cards: None.

Yellow card: Hoedt (62) ungentlemanly conduct.

Referee: Neil Swarbrick (Preston).

Attendance: 30,564.

match stats

ALBION		SOUTHAMPTON
2	Shots on target	5
1	Shots off target	5
2	Corners	7
0	Offside	1
9	Free-kicks against	10
52	Possession	48

referee

Neil Swarbrick appeared to get bigger calls right, such as the free-kick for Southampton's goal and yellow for Gaatan Bong as Saints asked for something more. But he was not always well assisted. **7**

next game

Swansea v Albion, Premier League, Saturday (3pm).

and table

Premier League

	P	W	D	L	F	A	Pts
Man City	10	9	1	0	35	6	28
Man Utd	10	7	2	1	23	4	23
Tottenham	10	6	2	2	19	7	20
Chelsea	10	6	1	3	18	10	19
Arsenal	10	6	1	3	19	13	19
Liverpool	10	4	4	2	17	16	16
Watford	10	4	3	3	15	18	15
Newcastle	9	4	2	3	10	8	14
Southampton	10	3	4	3	9	10	13
Burnley	9	3	4	2	8	9	13
Leicester	10	3	3	4	14	14	12
ALBION	10	3	3	4	10	11	12
Huddersfield	10	3	3	4	7	13	12
Stoke	10	3	2	5	11	20	11
West Brom	10	2	4	4	9	13	10
West Ham	10	2	3	5	10	19	9
Swansea	10	2	3	5	6	7	9
Everton	10	2	2	6	7	20	8
Bournemouth	10	2	1	7	6	14	7
Crystal Palace	10	1	1	8	4	21	4

yond the far post, planted a precise header into the roof of the net.

Fraser Forster really ought to have saved it. He could not shuffle his 6ft 6in frame across the line with sufficient speed and the ball was across the line before he got an airborne hand to it.

No matter, it was still a fine header and Murray has three goals in two games, the scoring touch he had in the Championship rediscovered now that he is approaching a return to peak fitness after ankle trouble.

Gross has been a bargain revelation in the No.10 role since his £3 million move from Ingolstadt, relegated from the Bundesliga.

He now has five assists in ten games to accompany two goals against West Brom and the free-kick which led to Tomer Hemed's winner against Newcastle.

That is some impact, and in addition to that, he has an insatiable work ethic.

Hughton said: "Particularly second half, the tempo of our game was very good. When you go 1-0 down so early against a team that maybe are not having the season they would have liked but have so much quality, credit to our lads for the way they responded. We thoroughly deserved to get back in the game.

"Everyone knows the circumstances against Everton. If it had been the other way around, we had scored first and then conceded, it's a little bit of a different feeling.

"The feeling is we showed great character to come back into the game, get the goal and probably finished the stronger team."

They might not have been accumulated in the anticipated order but five points from Everton, West Ham and Southampton will do nicely.

Congratulations on a fantastic season. Up the Albion!

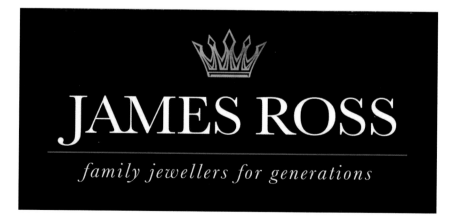

Albion ratings ✔

MATHEW RYAN
Hughton felt he made a difference when Narsingh hit the bar. But the save from Abraham and his footwork were more obvious. **7**

BRUNO
Shone with a defensive style as much about preventing danger as clearing it up. Good use of the ball is key to that. **8**

SHANE DUFFY
Dived in to help block in a scramble as part of a highly combative performance in a country which he is coming to love. **8**

LEWIS DUNK
Did well in the battle of the England hopefuls and nearly scored. Played more than half the game on a booking. **8**

GAETAN BONG
Dyer and later Narsingh offered a good outlet down Bong's side but, helped by the former's woeful end product, he was solid. **7**

ANTHONY KNOCKAERT
Back on the assist trail after his exploits in the Championship. Put Murray's goal on a plate. Bursts of intent, bit loose in possession at times. **7**

Lewis Dunk gave another solid display at centre-half in a clean sheet

DALE STEPHENS
No sign of a red card from Mike Dean this time and comfortable for him against lacklustre Swans. Just kept things ticking over. **7**

DAVY PROPPER
His cohesive partnership with Stephens upstaged Fer and the substituted Carroll for Swansea. Mobile Dutchman looks the part now. **7**

JOSE IZQUIERDO
Hughton demands his wingers work both ways. Colombian has engaged with that philosophy but few opportunities to shine going forward. **6**

PASCAL GROSS
Subdued by the German's high standards so far. No sign of an assist or goal to maintain his influence but still covered a lot of ground. **6**

GLENN MURRAY
Rich vein of scoring form goes on. If he keeps on getting the service, especially from wide areas, he will keep scoring. Adept penalty box predator. **7**

SUBS
SOLLY MARCH: Slotted in steadily.
TOMER HEMED: Brief return from ban.
IZZY BROWN: Late replacement for Gross.

Seagulls flying

September fears seem a distant memory

Swansea.....0
Albion..........1

WHO would have believed it on September 1?

Even the most optimistic Albion supporter could not possibly have envisaged them entering the third international break in such a healthy state.

Not when they approached the first with one point and no goals in three games and without the extra striker they were desperate to sign in the transfer window.

The managerial acumen of Chris Hughton, coupled with the desire of players – both the existing core and those added from abroad – to prove they can cut it in the Premier League has produced an improbable set of results and position inside the top ten.

Since the early setbacks and fears, they have lost just twice in eight matches, won four of them, including consecutive clean sheet victories away from the Amex, where they were expected to struggle.

Yes, it is too soon to get carried away, especially with a demanding spell on the horizon until the transfer window re-opens in the New Year, but the platform to achieve the goal of survival has sound foundations.

Hughton, reflecting on the progress made from apparent adversity, said: "We have players that have come in and very much bought in to the way we play.

"Some have played a big part, others less, but at the moment we have got a very competitive squad.

"You want to get the best out of the players you've got and they couldn't give me any more at the moment.

"It's common knowledge we were looking to bring in a striker but we're not the only club. Sometimes it happens and it wouldn't be the first time or the first window that we've missed out on players.

"The good thing always about the first of September is once that day comes everybody knuckles down and does the best they can."

The first striker Albion wanted in the summer was Tammy Abraham. As he trudged off the pitch to applause at the Liberty Stadium, long after his team-mates had disappeared down the tunnel to a chorus of boos, the on-loan Chelsea prospect must have wished he had chosen differently.

A player with his transparent talent, acknowledged by Gareth Southgate with an England call-up, deserves better. Swansea were

Anthony Knockaert races past Ki Sung-Yueng of Swansea at the Liberty Stadium

Full-back Gaetan Bong tackles Nathan Dyer

Shane Duffy and Jordan Ayew

By ANDY NAYLOR
Chief sports reporter

dreadful. One of the concerns at the start of the season was trying to identify three teams Albion could finish above.

The Welshmen, even with 81 points still to play for, definitely warrant that ranking.

They were worse than West Ham, even though Albion beat them 3-0. The Hammers produced a response to Glenn Murray's early header until Jose Izquierdo killed their resolve just before half-time.

Swansea? Abraham apart, they offered very little. No pressure on the ball, no confidence and, on this evidence, no hope of survival.

A toxic atmosphere did not help. You could sense the anxiety of their disgruntled supporters, witnessing a fifth home defeat, from the outset.

That is no excuse, however, at this level for the degree of incompetence displayed. On a handful of occasions in the second half, short and mid-range free-kicks and passes went straight out of play. Incredible.

in face of adversity

Glenn Murray steers the ball home with his thigh from Anthony Knockaert's cross to give Albion victory

Sting was sending out an SOS through the loudspeakers at the end. It was an appropriate epitaph for Swansea's ineptitude.

Even so, take nothing away from Hughton and his players. Another thoroughly professional away performance, based on solid defending and a moment of quality, was sufficient.

Anthony Knockaert jinked back on to his left foot to deliver the type of cross Glenn Murray devours. He did so, from point-blank range, with his thigh for his fourth goal in three games, elevating him to equality with Abraham's tally.

It completed a horrible minute for Federico Fernandez, the Swansea skipper. Rightly booked by Mike Dean for going through Murray from behind on the halfway line, the hapless Argentinian was then statuesque as Knockaert's cross flew over him. Albion were only twice in jeopardy of relinquishing their third clean sheet in six matches.

Early in the second half Mathew Ryan smothered Abraham, the one serious save needed from the Australian. In stoppage time, substitute Luciano Narsingh, fed by Abraham, struck the crossbar.

It would have been a terrible waste of two points if that had gone in.

Hughton said: "It's certainly better going into the break on the back of a win. That feel lasts a bit longer.

"We've been very good for the last two seasons.

"I've seen players improve their game and play at a really good standard.

"I'm really delighted they are getting the opportunity now to do that at Premier League level."

They are seizing it so far with both hands.

the teams

Albion (4-4-1-1): Ryan; Bruno, Duffy, Dunk, Bong; Knockaert, Stephens, Propper, Izquierdo; Gross; Murray.

Subs: March for Izquierdo (65), Hemed for Murray (78), Brown for Gross (85), Krul, Suttner, Goldson, Schelotto.

Goals: Murray (29).

Red cards: None.

Yellow card: Dunk (foul).

Swansea (4-1-2-3): Fabianski; Naughton, Mawson, Fernandez, Clucas; Ki sung-yuen; Fer, Carroll; Dyer, Abraham, Ayew.

Subs: Narsingh for Carroll (59), McBurnie for Ayew (79), Routledge for Clucas (79), Nordfeldt, van der Hoorn, Mesa, Fulton.

Goals: None.

Red cards: None.

Yellow cards: Fernandez (foul), Clucas (dissent).

Referee: Mike Dean (Wirral).

Attendance: 20,822.

match stats

ALBION		SWANSEA
2	Shots on	2
3	Shots off	8
7	Corners	8
2	Offsides	1
12	Free-kicks against	13
44	Possession	56

Lewis Dunk offers to help up Tammy Abraham

referee

Had it not been for what has gone before, Mike Dean would have gone almost unnoticed. An unremarkable afternoon. **7**

next up

Albion v Stoke, Premier League, Monday November 20 (8pm).

and table

Premier League

	P	W	D	L	F	A	Pts
Man City	11	10	1	0	38	7	31
Man Utd	11	7	2	2	23	5	23
Tottenham	11	7	2	2	20	7	23
Chelsea	11	7	1	3	19	10	22
Liverpool	11	5	4	2	21	17	19
Arsenal	11	6	1	4	20	16	19
Burnley	11	5	4	2	10	9	19
ALBION	11	4	3	4	11	11	15
Watford	11	4	3	4	17	21	15
Huddersfield	11	4	3	4	8	13	15
Newcastle	11	4	2	5	10	10	14
Leicester	11	3	4	4	16	16	13
Southampton	11	3	4	4	9	11	13
Stoke	11	3	3	5	13	22	12
Everton	11	3	2	6	10	22	11
West Brom	11	2	4	5	9	14	10
Bournemouth	11	3	1	7	7	14	10
West Ham	11	2	3	6	11	23	9
Swansea	11	2	2	7	7	13	8
Crystal Palace	11	1	1	9	4	22	4

MATHEW RYAN 7/10

Kept Albion in the game with his block from Sobhi at 2-1 and tipped over from Shawcross. Cleverly wrong-footed by Choupo-Moting on the first goal.

BRUNO 6/10

Some decent defending at times but also a misjudgement on the second Stoke goal as turned his back on the ball.

SHANE DUFFY 6/10

Arguably the most solid of the defensive unit although the collective was not as watertight this time as it has been.

LEWIS DUNK 6/10

Caught out by the magic of Shaqiri and the movement of Choupo-Moting for the first goal. Generally decent enough.

GAETAN BONG 6/10

Did his bit defensively but unable to make things happen going the other way as he sometimes can.

ANTHONY KNOCKAERT 6/10

No magical moment to crown his 26th birthday despite plenty of good intentions. Taken off for the final push.

DALE STEPHENS 7/10

Another decent offering. Started in great style, popping the ball about and sending a fierce long-ranger just wide.

DAVY PROPPER 7/10

Inspired work to create room for himself and cross for the first home goal. Might have done better with a header earlier.

JOSE IZQUIERDO 7/10

You never quite know what he is going to do but he excited and showed great reactions and control to guide his side level for a second time.

PASCAL GROSS 7/10

Back on the goal trail with a shot which Grant might have saved. Tried to make thing happen but looked tired when replaced late on.

GLENN MURRAY 7/10

No record-breaking goal but a really clever, battling display quite apart from the incident which should have brought a penalty.

SUBS
Solly March: Ruffled a few feathers and worried Diouf.
Ezequiel Schelotto: Got himself into one great position which he wasted with the cross.
Izzy Brown: Battled away in the final stages.

Seagulls show

Albion hit back twice to earn a vital point

 Albion..........2
 Stoke...........2

YOU have to show character to survive in the Premier League – and Albion possess it in abundance.

They came from behind twice, Pascal Gross and Jose Izquierdo cancelling out goals for Stoke by Maxim Choupo-Moting and Kurt Zouma in an entertaining match.

Chris Hughton's side also recovered from a goal down to take a point in the previous home against Southampton.

That is three draws in a row at the Amex, where the Seagulls were expected to gain most of their points.

The script is being re-written somewhat following successive away wins at West Ham and Swansea but Albion are entitled to feel a little aggrieved on this occasion.

Referee Lee Mason denied them a blatant penalty in the first half when they were 1-0 behind and Ryan Shawcross brought down Glenn Murray.

Although Albion have suffered their fair share of injury problems this season, Hughton was able to name the same starting line-up for the fourth game in succession.

That is a comforting situation for any manager and a reflection of how consistently the team has been performing – but it is bound to alter, last night's encounter launching a hectic spell of 11 matches in six weeks up to Bournemouth's visit on New Year's Day.

Gaetan Bong made his 50th appearance for the club in a defence which had conceded only one goal in the previous three games.

The switch by Mark Hughes to a back three for Stoke this season has been plagued by injury troubles. They have been more settled of late but a broken finger sustained by Jack Butland in training on England duty forced a change in goal, as Lee Grant made his first Premier League appearance since April.

Dale Stephens, such an influence in the centre of the park for Albion, started the match particularly well, spreading the play on a zippy pitch and emphasising the confidence of a player in form with a shot from distance which whistled a yard wide.

The Seagulls exploited a glaring weakness in the Stoke set-up. Mame Diouf, a striker converted into a right-wingback, was caught out of position several times, which allowed Izquierdo acres of space.

The Colombian left-winger nearly put Albion ahead in the 17th minute, running onto a Davy Propper pass and cutting inside onto his favoured right foot to fire just

Pascal Gross drills home in the first half to brings Albion level in the first half

Glenn Murray is felled by Ryan a Shawcross challenge

Maxim Choupo-Moting fires Stoke ahead against Albion in the first half

Pictures: Simon Dack/Liz Finlayson

By ANDY NAYLOR
Chief sports reporter

wide of the far post.

Albion did not have it all their own way. Mathew Ryan, fresh from qualifying for the World Cup finals with Australia, had to tip over a Shawcross header from Darren Fletcher's corner.

There was a further example of the defensive diligence which has served Albion well so far when Lewis Dunk produced a fine block from Xherdan Shaqiri's angled effort on the run after a slip by Propper.

Dunk, such a tower of strength with Shane Duffy, was uncharacteristically caught out when Stoke took the lead in the 28th minute.

Shaqiri was the architect, the diminutive Swiss international delivering a sublime ball over the top of Dunk for Choupo-Moting.

The German-born Cameroon international, on target twice in Stoke's home draw with Manchester United, took advantage of a helpful touch off Dunk to slot past Ryan.

Albion once again found themselves having to come from behind, just as they did to draw the last home game against Southampton.

They were denied a blatant

character in draw

Albion's Pascal Gross celebrates his goal against Stoke City at the Amex in the Premier League

penalty when Murray, after a neat combination with Gross, was brought down by Shawcross inside the box.

Shawcross was nowhere near the ball when he made contact with Murray with an outstretched leg, but referee Mason and his assistant let the Stoke skipper off the hook.

Not for long after Murray had been booked for a late challenge on Kevin Wimmer which smacked of frustration.

A remarkable diagonal run by Propper, evading several challenges, ended with the Dutchman crossing low for Gross to drill through the legs of Grant in the 44th minute.

Justice seemed to be done at that point but there was still time for Stoke to deflate the Seagulls by regaining the lead in first-half stoppage time.

Chelsea's on-loan French defender Zouma headed in from close range when the

defence failed to deal with another Fletcher corner.

Bruno was the culprit.

He was marking Choupo-Moting and not looking at the ball when it rebounded off the Spaniard's back obligingly for Zouma.

Neither defence looked comfortable. Albion's customary solidity deserted them and they were grateful to Ryan after slack play outside their own penalty area early in the second half.

Ramadan Sobhi ex-

changed passes with Joe Allen before Ryan, rushing off his line, blocked the Egyptian international's effort with his chest at close quarters.

The value of Ryan's intervention was highlighted as Albion restored parity again on the hour, courtesy of poor Stoke defending.

Murray latched onto Zouma's indecisive header to feed Izquierdo.

He tucked in his first goal at the Amex from a tight an-

gle after the ball rebounded back to him from his first attempt off Wimmer.

Both managers made changes in search of a winner.

Hughton introduced Solly March, Izzy Brown and Ezequiel Schelotto. For Stoke, Peter Crouch's 143rd substitute appearance created a new Premier League record.

They had to settle in the end for a hard-earned and eventful point apiece.

Albion ratings

MATHEW RYAN
Did the little that was asked with superb double save on half-time to deny Lukaku and Pogba. No chance with United's fortunate winner. **8/10**

BRUNO
Linked well with Knockaert in first half and no repeat of mishaps defending set pieces against Everton and Stoke. Martial made no impact. **8/10**

SHANE DUFFY
Back to the towering form he has displayed all season. Only blemish a booking for upending Ibrahimovic, leaving him on the brink of a ban. **8/10**

LEWIS DUNK
Like Duffy, a return to high standards after slight dip against Stoke. Very unfortunate with the goal. Might have made amends soon after. **8/10**

GAETAN BONG
Whether it is March or Izquierdo in front of him, solid as a rock. Mata, then Rashford, were both ineffective on the United right and were replaced. **8/10**

ANTHONY KNOCKAERT
Best game of the season? He was a bundle of energy and aggressive in his attacking ideas. Just lacking that bit of precision at key moments. **8/10**

Pascal Gross fires in a cross

DALE STEPHENS
Busy looking to keep an eye on Pogba's promptings. Tried to be constructive with passes but that led to a couple of losses of possession. **7/10**

DAVY PROPPER
Hard working, looking to close spaces and then give a simple pass. Great to see him striding forward into the box in the first half. **7/10**

SOLLY MARCH
Back in the side and had a couple of forays early on. Much of his time was spent tracking back, including that key moment before the goal. **7/10**

PASCAL GROSS
Lots of movement into good areas. His turn to set up a chance will stay in the memory but might have done better when teed up by Bruno. **8/10**

GLENN MURRAY
Sterling work by the frontman. Held the ball, troubled defenders and forced free-kicks. A shame that back-heel flick did not come off. **8/10**

SUBS
JOSE IZQUIERDO: A useful option late on and got on the ball a few times to no avail.
TOMER HEMED: Not much chance to shine, even though Albion were pushing on.
IZZY BROWN: Sent on late.

Albion are up

Top-half credentials on show - but no luck

 Man Utd.......1
 Albion..........0

ALBION are in the top ten of the Premier League on merit.

Nobody can doubt that after an unlucky 13th game at Old Trafford.

Their performance warranted the distinction of being the first team to take away a point this season.

Only a goal laced with controversy and misfortune deprived them.

Here was further evidence that Albion are growing and developing.

They looked every inch a highly competitive and competent Premier League outfit.

A relieved Jose Mourinho was effusive in his praise afterwards, although it is easier to be complimentary when you have under-performed and nicked a win.

United were subdued and lacklustre. Midweek Champions League duty was no excuse, because Mourinho made seven changes to the team beaten in Basel.

On this evidence the gap between them and neighbours City at the top of the table flatters them.

Albion's display, meanwhile, emphasised their continued improvement since losing at home to City on the opening day and at Arsenal last month.

Chris Hughton agreed. He said: "Yes, even though in both of those games which we lost 2-0 I was pleased with more than I was unhappy with.

"Out of the three this was the best. We've gone another step forward, to do that at Old Trafford."

Hughton suffered a 3-0 defeat with Newcastle, a 4-0 defeat with Norwich, on his previous visits as a manager.

There was never the remotest danger of losing as comprehensively again.

He made an astute tactical adjustment by moving Davy Propper slightly further forward in the middle of the park alongside Pascal Gross, with Dale Stephens sitting behind them.

The Dutchman and German saw plenty of the ball, and there was no shortage of adventure, particularly in the first half, when opportunities arose to push forward.

If there was a disappointment, Albion had plenty of promising situations and 'maybe moments' but no clear chance to avert a fifth blank sheet.

That remains the only slight concern, whether they can score

United take the lead through Ashley Young's deflected shot as Lewis Dunk gets an unfortunate touch

Shane Duffy cannot believe he has headed wide late on

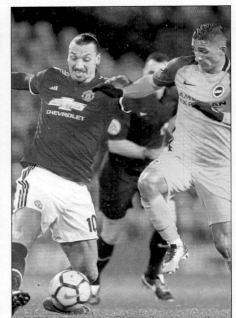
Zlatan Ibrahimovic with Anthony Knockaert

BY ANDY NAYLOR
Chief sports reporter

enough goals to maintain a comfortable position, free of relegation worries.

Hughton said: "That's the ultimate I suppose. We defended well, blocking holes, worked our way into really good areas, and then scoring at the end of it is everything.

"It's difficult to have everything for a club like ours coming here, to have that perfect performance.

"If we were able to finish off a couple of chances then that would have been a perfect performance."

It was more or less perfect in a defensive sense, considering the attacking power at Mourinho's disposal.

He started with Romelu Lukaku, Marcus Rashford and Juan Mata, brought on Zlatan Ibrahimovic, Henrikh Mkhitaryan and Marouane Fellaini.

Yet Mathew Ryan was only called upon twice, in the same incident, to save Albion.

That was on the stroke of half-

where they belong

Albion goalkeeper Mathew Ryan is ready to save as Romelu Lukaku heads for goal from close range. **Pictures by Richard Parkes**

the teams

Albion (4-1-2-3): Ryan; Bruno, Duffy, Dunk, Bong; Stephens; Propper, Gross; Knockaert, Murray, March.
Subs: Hemed for Murray (74), Izquierdo for March (74), Brown for Gross (88), Krul, Goldson, Schelotto, Kayal.
Goals: None.
Yellow cards: Murray (58) foul, Duffy (87) foul.
Manchester United (4-2-3-1): De Gea; Valencia, Smalling, Lindelof, Young; Matic, Pogba; Mata, Rashford, Martial; Lukaku.
Subs: Ibrahimovic for Mata (61), Mkhitaryan for Martial (70), Fellaini for Rashford (80), Rojo, Romero, Herrera, McTominay.
Goals: Dunk own goal (66).
Yellow cards: None.
Referee: Neil Swarbrick (Lancs).
Attendance: 75,018 (approx 3,000 away).

stats

ALBION		MAN UTD
2	On target	6
4	Off target	11
0	Corners	5
1	Offsides	1
9	Free-kicks against	9

ref watch

Neil Swarbrick kept a lid on one or two potential flashpoints and rightly waved way penalty claims against Dunk (foul) and Fellaini (handball). His assistant did very well on the corner verdict for the goal but should he have flagged for Lukaku's subsequent clash with Bong. **7**

next up

Albion v Crystal Palace, Premier League, tomorrow, 7.45pm.

and table

Premier League

	P	W	D	L	F	A	Pts
Man City	13	12	1	0	42	8	37
Man Utd	13	9	2	2	28	6	29
Chelsea	13	8	2	3	24	11	26
Arsenal	13	8	1	4	23	16	25
Tottenham	13	7	3	3	21	10	24
Liverpool	13	6	5	2	25	18	23
Burnley	13	6	4	3	12	10	22
Watford	13	6	3	4	22	21	21
ALBION	13	4	4	5	13	14	16
Southampton	13	4	4	5	13	15	16
Huddersfield	13	4	3	6	9	19	15
Leicester	13	3	5	5	17	19	14
Bournemouth	13	4	2	7	11	14	14
Newcastle	13	4	2	7	11	17	14
Stoke	13	3	4	6	16	26	13
Everton	13	3	3	7	13	28	12
West Brom	13	2	5	6	10	19	11
West Ham	13	2	4	7	12	26	10
Swansea	13	2	3	8	7	15	9
Crystal Palace	13	2	2	9	8	25	8

time, when the Australian pulled off a stunning double save.

He blocked Lukaku's header four yards out from Rashford's cross, then kept out Pogba's follow-up from point blank range with his left leg.

The goal that decided an even contest midway through the second half was cruel in the extreme.

Solly March, recalled in place of Jose Izquierdo, was convinced Albion should have been awarded a goalkick when Lukaku harried him.

The assistant indicated otherwise and referee Neil Swarbrick gave a corner, correctly as it transpired from footage on Match Of The Day.

When it eventually reached Ashley Young, Lewis Dunk threw himself at the shot 20 yards out in a trademark attempt to block. The ball looped off Dunk into the top left-hand corner of Ryan's net.

The United faithful must have expected the floodgates to open in the final quarter once they were in front. They were mistaken.

Anthony Knockaert, much livelier than of late, and Bruno flashed crosses across the edge of the six-yard box. Dunk, with a touch more composure at the vital moment, might have equalised after marauding forward to combine with Glenn Murray.

If Albion perform at the level they have in almost every game then the sequence of draws at the Amex has a good chance of coming to an end against Crystal Palace tomorrow.

MATHEW RYAN 8/10

Becoming the specialist of the double save – Everton, United and now this. Denied Benteke but the follow-up stop from Zaha was scarcely believable.

BRUNO 7/10

Good in defence bar of one free-kick concession and thoughtful in his passing. Tried too pick out a colleague on one notable occasion he got to the byline.

SHANE DUFFY 7/10

His far-post presence at set-pieces was a potential threat and he headed just over. Central defence was exposed once, when Ryan rescued his side

LEWIS DUNK 7/10

Generally in control, bar that moment which brought the double save. Booked for a shirt tug on one occasion Zaha gave him the slip.

MARKUS SUTTNER 7/10

Restored to defence through Bong's injury and looked keen to make an impact. Was tidy but could not provide the killer cross.

ANTHONY KNOCKAERT 7/10

Got through a huge amount of work with and without the ball and created danger at times but magic moment was missing.

DALE STEPHENS 6/10

A mixed evening with his passing – and shooting. Went close to a winner from long range in the second half.

DAVY PROPPER 6/10

Not a bad game. Saw plenty of the ball and tried to stretch play with his passing but not always to good effect.

JOSE IZQUIERDO 6/10

A bundle of energy down the left, going in both directions and keen to put in a defensive shift. Found room to test the diving Hennessey.

PASCAL GROSS 6/10

Tried all he could to find space and create a winner. But lacked power when he got the chance to test Hennessey with a first-half shot.

GLENN MURRAY 6/10

Kept so quiet by his old club until his final contribution, when he made space for himself and had a header cleared off the line.

SUBS

Solly March: Sent on to try and add spark on the left. 6
Izzy Brown: Battled but lacked invention.
Tomer Hemed: Never really get into the game

Bragging rights are shared with arch rivals

 Albion..........0
 C Palace......0

AS OFTEN happens, the hype up-staged the reality.

The first top flight clash between Albion and their fierce rivals since 1981 ended in an uninspiring stale-mate.

Palace boss Roy Hodgson, trying to steer them off the foot of the Premier League table, will be happier with the point, their first away from home this season.

For Chris Hughton, that is four home draws in succession for his Albion side, who looked a little jaded in their third match in the space of nine days.

Hughton will take satisfaction from the clean sheet which stretched Palace's run without an away goal to seven games, equalling a Premier League record.

Hughton made two amendments to his line-up, both on the left.

Markus Suttner returned to the defence for Gaetan Bong, who is nursing a knee niggle.

Record signing Jose Izquierdo was preferred ahead of the Austrian to Solly March.

Palace, buoyed by Saturday's last-gasp 2-1 home win over Stoke, handed fit-again Christian Benteke his first start since September at the expense of James McArthur.

Benteke had Wilfried Zaha playing off him to test the dependable defensive combination of Lewis Dunk and Shane Duffy.

The Albion duo were grateful to Mathew Ryan for preventing the visitors from seizing the initiative in the 14th minute.

The Australian keeper produced a remarkable double save just before half-time in Saturday's unfortunate 1-0 defeat at Manchester United.

Ryan repeated the feat when Benteke and Zaha linked up menacingly through the middle.

He parried Benteke's right-foot toe-poke from 12 yards, then recovered rapidly to smother Zaha's attempt to guide in the follow-up.

Palace looked the more cohesive side in the opening quarter of the contest.

Albion struggled to get Izquierdo and Anthony Knockaert, up against former Leicester teammate Jeffrey Schlupp down the other flank, on the ball.

Their first threat, midway through the first half, was via a set-piece, Dunk heading a Pascal Gross corner straight at Wayne Hennessey.

The match was not living up to its billing at that stage. Space was predictably tight and, Ryan's double rescue act apart, the teams largely cancelled one another out.

Albion put together a promising move in the 28th minute.

Glenn Murray gets a hug as the honours are shared after a hard-fought but goalless draw

Glenn Murray and Shane Duffy combine to clear a corner for the Seagulls

Jose Izquierdo fires in a shot for the Seagulls in a game of few chances

By ANDY NAYLOR
Chief sports reporter

Davy Propper and Suttner released Izquierdo to cut inside, his favourite ploy, for an angled drive which was beaten away by Wales international Hennessey.

The ball landed 20 yards out to Dale Stephens, who sliced his shot horribly wide.

Little had been seen of Gross, Albion's chief archtiect.

That changed when the German No.10 started a break by freeing Izquierdo.

Knockaert was up in support and so was Gross, demonstrating once more his high energy levels, but the shot lacked the necessary power to beat Hennessey.

It was indicative of an opening 45 minutes which simmered without ever coming to the boil. The only fireworks were let off in the away end by Palace supporters.

Both sides were sloppy on the resumption, repeatedly giving away possession cheaply.

An audacious attempt by Dunk to break the deadlock with a back-heel from another Gross corner to the near post brushed the side netting.

The game was in desperate need of a spark from somewhere to lift a suffocating stalemate in

quickly turn corner

Lewis Dunk and Steve Mounie
battle for the ball
Picture: Mike Egerton

the teams

Albion (4-4-1-1): Ryan; Bruno, Duffy, Dunk, Suttner; Schelotto, Stephens, Propper, Brown; Gross; Murray.
Subs: March for Schelotto (46), Izquierdo for Gross (63), Hemed for Brown (73), Krul, Huenemeier, Kayal, Baldock.
Goals: None.
Red cards: None.
Yellow cards: None.
Huddersfield (4-2-3-1): Lossl; Smith, Zanka, Schindler, Lowe; Mooy, Hogg; Quaner, Ince, Kachunga; Mounie.
Subs: Depoitre for Mounie (85), Lolley for Ince (86), Williams for Kachunga (89), Coleman, Whitehead, Cranie, Hadergjonaj.
Goals: Mounie (12) and (43).
Red cards: None.
Yellow cards: None.
Referee: Stuart Attwell (Warwickshire).
Attendance: 24,018.

stats

ALBION		HUDDERSFIELD
2	Shots on	6
5	Shots off	13
1	Corners	8
5	Offsides	1
10	Free-kicks conceded	6
59%	Possession	41%

referee

Stuart Attwell did not have major flashpoints to deal with

Not the toughest game to referee. It's hard to remember any real flashpoints for Stuart Attwell to deal with – and his assistants got the various offside decisions right. 7

next up

Spurs v Albion, Premier League, Wednesday, Wembley (8pm).

and table

Premier League

	P	W	D	L	F	A	Pts
Man City	16	15	1	0	48	11	46
Man Utd	16	11	2	3	36	11	35
Chelsea	16	10	2	4	28	13	32
Liverpool	16	8	6	2	34	20	30
Arsenal	16	9	2	5	30	20	29
Tottenham	16	8	4	4	28	14	28
Burnley	16	8	4	4	15	12	28
Leicester	16	6	5	5	23	22	23
Watford	16	6	4	6	25	27	22
Everton	16	5	4	7	20	29	19
Southampton	16	4	6	6	16	19	18
Huddersfield	16	5	3	8	11	26	18
ALBION	16	4	6	6	16	19	18
Bournemouth	16	4	4	8	15	19	16
Stoke	16	4	4	8	19	35	16
Newcastle	16	4	3	9	16	25	15
West Brom	16	2	7	7	12	22	13
West Ham	16	3	4	9	14	32	13
Swansea	16	3	3	10	9	18	12
Crystal Palace	16	2	5	9	10	27	11

have gone away with the match ball but scooped a second-half chance over the bar.

Hughton's selection came under contrasting scrutiny from supporters. He awarded Ezequiel Schelotto his first Premier League start at the expense of Anthony Knockaert, who was left out altogether.

Markus Suttner also returned at left-back in place of Gaetan Bong, who struggles to play three games in a week due to a knee issue.

It did not help that Schelotto resembled a fish out of water and was hooked at half-time but Hughton was right to point out his choices had nothing to do with the soft manner in which the goals were given away.

Knockaert has not been setting the world alight this season. Even in the Championship, where he was top dog, the Frenchman generally performed better at the Amex than away from home. Solly March, who took over from Schelotto for the second half, and record buy Jose Izquierdo, who scored Albion's last goal from open play against Stoke four-

and-a-third games ago, have also not been in the best of form lately.

The real difficulty for Hughton is that performance levels throughout the team, Old Trafford apart, have dropped a notch or two since the last win at Swansea prior to the international break.

The run of fixtures Albion are in now always looked tough on paper and that is the way it is panning out. It is not a cause for panic – periods like this were inevitable and others in the congested bottom half of the table are on bad runs too – but a re-

sumption of reliable defending and degree of attacking vigour cannot come quickly enough. Especially with Hughton's old club Tottenham lying in wait on Wednesday at Wembley, where they returned to form by destroying Stoke.

The absence of any meaningful response in the second half to a difficult but not insurmountable deficit was disturbing.

Leaking cheaply at one end and not looking like scoring at the other is a damaging combination, fatal if it continues.

Albion ratings ✓

MATHEW RYAN 7/10
A typically accomplished performance in wet conditions. Beaten in freak style for the opener when he seemed to have everything covered.

EZEQUIEL SCHELOTTO 7/10
Given a first league start at right-back and, after a nightmare first minute, settled in well, defending in athletic style and getting forward when he could.

SHANE DUFFY 7/10
Twice headed straight at Lloris with rare on-target Albion attempts but most of the evening was spent getting stuck into one of the toughest defensive assignments in the business

LEWIS DUNK 7/10
A hard-working evening as skipper against Spurs' feared attack and emerged with head held high. No treasured clean sheet but battled away well.

GAETAN BONG 7/10
The returning left-back competed well and looked to counter but got very lucky when Son sneaked in behind him and blazed over from very close range.

ANTHONY KNOCKAERT 7/10
Back in the side and looked hungry to run at opponents. Combined quite well with Schelotto and always looked the best chance of posing a counter-attack threat.

DALE STEPHENS 6/10
One of three central midfielders and given the job to block passing options, which happened, and keep the ball, which Albion did not do so well.

DAVY PROPPER 6/10
Dragged a shot wide in a reasonable position the second half but otherwise all about getting a foot in. Was too far off Son when the latter scored the second via his back.

BERAM KAYAL 6/10
A long-awaited taste of Premier League life as Albion looked for more midfield energy and one of which he can be proud. His tenacity set up Hemed's good chance.

JOSE IZQUIERDO 5/10
Albion looked to get him in behind Aurier but it did not work out – and tables were turned when the home full-back beat him en route to his freak opener.

TOMER HEMED 6/10
Could have crowned his evening in glory had his left-foot snapshot gone either side of Lloris. Until then, tried to get hold of the ball and keep it in his role as lone striker.

SUBS
Solly March: Added dynamism to the left-hand side but his delivery needed more precision. 6
Glenn Murray: Didn't get into the game.
Pascal Gross: Not much seen of him.

Luck's out for

Fluke goal puts Spurs on way to home win

 Tottenham..2
 Albion.........0

By ANDY NAYLOR
Chief sports reporter

CHRIS HUGHTON remarked before the clash against his old club that you can sometimes be satisfied after a game you have lost by the manner of the performance.

That was the case for the Albion manager at Wembley last night as a much-changed team produced a much-improved performance after the tame effort at Huddersfield.

A stuttering Spurs, although worthy winners, did not put the game to bed until doubling their lead two minutes from the end.

It was a spirited display by the Seagulls, who have now lost four of their last five matches and need a return to winning ways against in-form Burnley at the Amex at the weekend.

Hughton responded to the lacklustre 2-0 defeat at Huddersfield with five changes, freshening up the side and giving regulars a break before Saturday's third game in a week at home to the Clarets.

He changed both full-backs. Gaetan Bong was restored in place of Markus Suttner on the left and, with skipper Bruno among those rested, Ezequiel Schelotto reverted to right-back following an ineffective 45 minutes on the right side of midfield in Yorkshire.

The returns of Anthony Knockaert and Jose Izquierdo on the flanks and a first Premier League appearance for Beram Kayal in midfield after breaking a leg pre-season added energy and mobility to the line-up. Tomer Hemed led the line, with Glenn Murray, Pascal Gross and Izzy Brown joining Bruno among the subs and Suttner left out of the 18 altogether.

Mauricio Pochettino also changed both full-backs in four amendments to the Tottenham team that thrashed Stoke 5-1 on Saturday. Serge Aurier and Danny Rose came in for Kieran Trippier and Ben Davies. Pochetttino also brought fellow Argentinian Erik Lamela and Moussa Sissoko into the midfield and attacking mix for Mousa Dembele and Dele Alli.

Albion narrowly avoided an early setback when Shane Duffy, having partially headed clear, made a lunging challenge on Heung-Min Son inside the penalty area.

The Irishman connected with the ball before bringing down the South Korean and referee Bobby Madley decided correctly not to award a spot-kick, although it was a close call.

The tone was soon set, the Seagulls dropping into a 4-5-1 formation out of possession, which was most of the time. The idea was to hit Spurs on the counter and they had one or two promising moments in this respect, especially when Knockaert instigated a move involving several players.

It ended with Schelotto's header dropping too far behind Izquierdo, who could only hook a volley high over the bar.

Hughton was entitled to be satisfied with the opening quarter of the contest. Spurs dominated the ball without fashioning much.

It was certainly an improvement on Huddersfield.

Son, who terrorised Stoke, should have put Spurs ahead in the 24th minute. Harry Kane flicked on a cross to him at the far post, where the Asian winger lifted the ball over the bar from close range.

The Seagulls took the opportunity to slow the game down at every opportunity, Mathew Ryan taking his time with goalkicks and his team-mates likewise from throwins. This annoyed the home supporters, who were also agitated by Tottenham's failure to find a way through and some errant passes.

Lamela, making his first start for 14 months following hip trouble, fired over on the turn inside the box after Kane made a nuisance of himself.

Albion needed to be better on the ball when they had it to provide occasional relief. They managed to force a corner, their first, in the 36th minute. Duffy rose to meet Knockaert's delivery but the header was straight at Hugo

Tottenham Hotspur's Son, centre, appeals for a penalty after a tackle from Albion's Shane Duffy

Harry Kane watches as Serge Aurier's cross sails over everyone and into the Albion goal

Spurs get their second goal in the closing stages at Wembley

Pictures: Simon Dack

Albion at Wembley

Gaetan Bong flies through the air as he battles for the ball for the Seagulls

the teams

Tottenham (4-2-3-1): Lloris; Aurier, Dier, Vertonghen, Rose; Winks (Dembele 67), Sissoko; Lamela (Alli 74), Eriksen, Son (Davies 90); Kane.

Subs not used: Vorm, Trippier, Llorente, Foyth.

Goals: Aurier 41, Son 87.

Yellow card: Rose (45) foul.

Albion (4-5-1): Ryan; Schelotto, Duffy, Dunk, Bong; Knockaert, Stephens, Propper, Kayal (Gross 78), Izquierdo (March 62); Hemed (Murray 72).

Subs not used: Krul, Bruno, Goldson, Brown.

Yellow card: Knockaert (41) dissent.

Attendance: 46,438 (approx. 3,000 away).

stats

ALBION		SPURS
4	Shots on	7
3	Shots off	17
2	Corners	10
0	Offsides	2
10	Free-kicks conceded	5
25	Possession	75

Jose Izquierdo tries to break forward for the Seagulls

ref watch

Bobby Madley: Easy to think of one referee who would have been celebrating the advantage Bobby Madley played when Aurier scored! Also did well to wave away penalty appeals when Duffy tackled Son. **8**

next up

Albion v Burnley, Premier League, Saturday, 3pm

and table

Premier League

	P	W	D	L	F	A	Pts
Man City	17	16	1	0	52	11	49
Man Utd	17	12	2	3	37	11	38
Chelsea	17	11	2	4	31	14	35
Tottenham	17	9	4	4	30	14	31
Liverpool	17	8	7	2	34	20	31
Burnley	17	9	4	4	16	12	31
Arsenal	17	9	3	5	30	20	30
Leicester	17	7	5	5	27	23	26
Watford	17	6	4	7	26	29	22
Everton	17	6	4	7	21	29	22
Southampton	17	4	6	7	17	23	18
Huddersfield	17	5	3	9	12	29	18
ALBION	**17**	**4**	**5**	**8**	**14**	**23**	**17**
Bournemouth	17	4	4	9	15	20	16
Stoke	17	4	4	9	19	36	16
Newcastle	17	4	3	10	16	26	15
West Brom	17	2	8	7	12	22	14
Crystal Palace	17	3	5	9	12	28	14
West Ham	17	3	5	9	14	32	14
Swansea	17	3	3	11	9	22	12

Lloris. That was the French keeper's first involvement, although by that time Ryan had not been seriously called upon either, which emphasised how disciplined Albion had been defensively.

Their solid work was undone in unfortunate manner four minutes from the interval. Right-back Aurier skipped away from Izquierdo close to the touchline. The Colombian fouled him as his cross sailed over Ryan into the net. The assistant flagged for Izquierdo's foul but the goal stood, referee Madley allowing a rapidly rewarded advantage.

Ivory Coast international Aurier's first club goal since scoring for Paris St Germain exactly two years ago ruined Albion's hopes of reaching half-time still on terms.

They were entitled to feel aggrieved by the method of Tottenham's goal. You need the rub of the green to get improbable results and Albion had no luck at Old Trafford last month either, when Manchester United fluked a winner with an Ashley Young shot deflected in by Lewis Dunk, Wembley skipper in the absence of Bruno.

Tottenham pressed with more purpose after the break in search of a second goal to kill the game. Ryan saved a Kane shot with his legs, then combined with Duffy to deny Son when he seemed sure to convert the rebound, although the assistant's flag had been raised for offside in any case.

Ryan also kept out a low drive by Lamela at the foot of his right-hand post to keep Albion in touch.

All the while it remained at 1-0 they retained hope, although there were few signs of them equalising. A break by Knockaert ended with Hemed shooting straight at Lloris on his first start since scoring the winner and incurring a restrospective suspension for a stamp against Newcastle in September.

With Solly March on for Izquierdo and causing goalscorer Aurier problems, Hemed spurned a good chance from 12 yards out, firing too close to Lloris after fellow countryman Kayal worked the ball to him.

After Ryan nudged a Kane free-kick onto the post, Spurs finally sealed Albion's fate two minutes from time, Son's stooping near post header from a Christian Eriksen free-kick deflecting in off Davy Propper.

Albion still so

Albion ratings ✓

MATHEW RYAN
Giving the keeper top mark does not do justice to the team display. But, equally, his saves (quality rather than quantity) deserve praise. **8/10**

BRUNO
Patient and precise on the ball as he tried to get moves rolling. Good defending as last man when Gudmundsson broke away on a counter. **7/10**

SHANE DUFFY
Error late on has cost him a fifth booking and a ban. Caused some problems by Wood and Vokes but got in a great block on the latter. **6/10**

LEWIS DUNK
Accomplished defending and use of the ball slightly tarnished when Wood, then Gudmundsson, got in down his side for good chances. **7/10**

GAETAN BONG
Looked like Cork and Gudmundsson would cause major problems down his side early on. Grew into the game but passing was hit and miss. **6/10**

ANTHONY KNOCKAERT
Desperately unlucky with volley against post and shot from acute angle deflected just wide of back stick. Gave Taylor awkward moments. **7/10**

Mathew Ryan made some good saves for Albion

DALE STEPHENS
Better on the ball than of late. Made a comfortable goal-line clearance but suffered a knock in the tackle for which he was booked. **7/10**

DAVY PROPPER
Got around the pitch to good effect and passing was more reliable than recently. Tame shot wide indicative of lack of goal threat. **7/10**

SOLLY MARCH
Decent return to the starting line-up, which was warranted. Good tussle with experienced Bardsley. Needs to improve final ball or shot. **6/10**

PASCAL GROSS
Nearly another assist with the cross for Knockaert's volley against the woodwork. Influence waned as the game wore on. **6/10**

GLENN MURRAY
Gave England-touted Tarkowski a tough time. Earned penalty and should have been awarded another. Slip on spot-kick unfortunate but Albion needed that to go in. **6/10**

SUBS
TOMER HEMED: Couldn't make headway.
IZZY BROWN: Chose wrong pass option a couple of times.
JOSE IZQUIERDO: Should have been booked for dive in box.

Seagulls must pick up those home wins

 Albion.........0
 Burnley.......0

ALBION are a whisker away from extricating themselves from the heavily populated fight for Premier League survival.

The worry is they are running out of realistic opportunities to gain the home wins which will be crucial to staying out of the bottom three.

Their record at the Amex is not bad. Only Manchester City and Liverpool have beaten them.

But 11 points from nine games is not good enough as a platform for safety.

Not when Chelsea, Arsenal, Spurs and Manchester United all visit in the second half of the season.

Home draws are hurting Albion badly. A fifth against Burnley, to accompany those against Everton, Southampton, Stoke and Crystal Palace, was scant reward for a much-improved performance which warranted all three points against the side currently breaking up the Big Six domination.

The table reveals how costly the spate of stalemates is proving to be.

Converting two of the five draws into victories would have Albion comfortably placed inside the top ten with Saturday's out-of-form visitors Watford.

The other home games that remain, against Bournemouth, West Ham, Swansea, Leicester and Huddersfield, are going to be vital.

Albion have already won twice away, which is unusually good for a promoted team at this stage.

It is at the Amex - where they have not won since September - that the fate of Chris Hughton's side is likely to be decided.

Hughton said: "We are playing against better opposition. That's what I have to keep stressing.

"I'd be more disappointed if we hadn't got some of the results away from home, because that's levelled it a little bit.

"But we have got to find a way of winning the games here and this was one of them.

"As good as Burnley are - and you can see at first hand why they are where they are, very well organised, can go back to front, can keep the ball in the final third - on the balance of play it's a game we lost out on."

Landing a striker in January who can run in behind and stretch defences - after missing out on one in the summer - could make all the difference.

Glenn Murray (No.17) sends his penalty over the bar as a golden chance goes begging for Albion

Lewis Dunk, left of picture, sees his header cleared off the line by Phil Bardsley

By ANDY NAYLOR
Chief sports reporter

Albion are too easy for Premier League defences to deal with. They have gone six-and-a-third games now without a goal from open play.

It is difficult to see them scoring much, other than from a set piece or mistake by their opponents.

Burnley obliged in this respect when James Tarkowski brought down Glenn Murray in a clumsy tangle of legs inside the box.

Murray, losing his footing slightly on his run-up, put the penalty straight down the middle and over the bar.

He is usually dependable from the spot. That is how the only goal came in the last six games, against Liverpool, along with the third which clinched the convincing win at West Ham.

Albion should have been awarded another penalty when Tarkowski elbowed Murray in the ribs but it was missed by referee Chris Kavanagh and his assistants.

The Seagulls are due some luck. Anthony Knockaert volleyed a

near and yet so far

Shane Duffy goes flying as Chris Wood nudges him in the back during Albion's goalless draw. Pictures by Liz Finlayson

Pascal Gross cross against a post and Lewis Dunk's header from a corner was nodded off the line by Phil Bardsley in a first half display among the best all season.

The danger of paying the price felt omnipresent, especially as Burnley have turned sitting in and nicking games into an art form.

Dale Stephens cleared a second half header from a Tarkowski header off the line to prevent Albion con-ceding from a corner yet again.

Mathew Ryan also denied ex-Seagull Chris Wood his sixth goal in as many starts against his former club when Dunk played him onside.

Hughton said: "I wanted, a better level of performance, because that's the only thing that gives us a chance of getting points.

"In recent games that has dipped, which has been disappointing, but we started well. We needed to. I

think it was always going to be a close game.

"Burnley don't have too many games that are not close affairs.

"A lot of the games they have won they have won 1-0, so we knew it would be close.

"We needed to score a goal in our good period of the game.

"The positives are a clean sheet, staying in there in the difficult part we had in the second half when

Maty made a good save, but for 70% of the game we were good value to have won."

Watford have only a point from their last four games, the same as Albion.

The teams are even on current form but the Seagulls could do with more than another even scoreline to make the turkey taste that bit more succulent.

the teams

Albion (4-1-4-1): Ryan; Bruno, Duffy, Dunk, Bong; Knockaert, Stephens, Propper, March; Gross; Murray.
Subs: Hemed for MurRay (63), Brown for Gross (74), Izquierdo for Knockaert (83), Krul, Kayal, Goldson, Schelotto.
Goals: None.
Red cards: None.
Yellow cards: March (68) foul, Stephens (77) foul, Dunk (87) foul, Duffy (90) handball.
Burnley (4-4-1-1): Pope; Bardsley, Mee, Tarkowski, Taylor; Gudmundsson, Defour, Cork, Arfield; Hendrick; Wood.
Subs: Barnes for Defour (68), Vokes for Wood (80), Lindegaard, Lowton, Westwood, Wells, Long.
Goals: None.
Red cards: None.
Yellow cards: Taylor (48) foul, Barnes (72) foul.
Attendance: 29,921 (1,422 away).
Referee: Chris Kavanagh (Lancs).

stats

ALBION		BURNLEY
2	On target	6
10	Off target	5
8	Corners	2
2	Offsides	1
13	Free-kicks against	13

ref watch

Chirs Kavanagh was the latest referee to come under trial by television due to incidents involving Tarkowski and Izquierdo. The latter deserved a booking and there were big question marks over key moments involving the former . **5**

next up

Albion v Watford, Premier League, Saturday (3pm).

and table

Premier League

	P	W	D	L	F	A	Pts
Man City	18	17	1	0	56	12	52
Man Utd	18	13	2	3	39	12	41
Chelsea	18	12	2	4	32	14	38
Liverpool	18	9	7	2	38	20	34
Arsenal	18	10	3	5	31	20	33
Burnley	18	9	5	4	16	12	32
Tottenham	18	9	4	5	31	18	31
Leicester	18	7	5	6	27	26	26
Watford	18	6	4	8	27	33	22
Everton	17	6	4	7	21	29	22
Huddersfield	18	6	3	9	16	30	21
Southampton	18	4	6	8	17	24	18
ALBION	**18**	**4**	**6**	**8**	**14**	**23**	**18**
Crystal Palace	18	4	5	9	15	28	17
West Ham	18	4	5	9	17	32	17
Bournemouth	18	4	4	10	15	24	16
Stoke	18	4	4	10	19	39	16
Newcastle	18	4	3	11	16	27	15
West Brom	18	2	8	8	13	24	14
Swansea	17	3	3	11	9	22	12

Brighton & Hove Albion 1 **Watford** **0**

Lewis Dunk, left, went close with this header while, right, Albion celebrate Pascal Gross' winner Pictures: Simon Dack

Christmas comes early

PASCAL GROSS fired home against Watford to secure Albion's first win in eight games – their first at the Amex since September – and bring early Christmas cheer.

German Gross rewarded a dominant performance by the Seagulls on Saturday with the only goal of the game in the 64th minute.

Hornets keeper Heurelho Gomes should have saved his shot, which ended a drought for the Seagulls in open play spanning ten hours and 34 minutes since Jose Izquierdo's second equaliser against Stoke, but it went under his body.

Defender Connor Goldson made his Premier League debut nine months after undergoing major heart surgery and impressed after stepping in for the suspended Shane Duffy.

Albion boss Chris Hughton said: "It's a happy changing room for Connor, because he's a very popular player.

"We all know what he went through."

Connor Goldson in action, above, on his Premier League debut and, centre, Pascal Gross celebrates after scoring, right

Welcome to our occasional feature You're In The Argus. Our photographers have been out and about capturing people and events around the county

PICTURES: SIMON DACK

Albion ratings ✓

MATTHEW RYAN
Did everything asked of him in tricky conditions for keepers. Foiled Alonso twice in quick succession before the wing-back struck. **8**

EZEQUIEL SCHELOTTO
Best 45 minutes in an Albion shirt in first half, deputising again for the rested Bruno. Prominent defensively inside his own box. **7**

SHANE DUFFY
Restored after one-match ban for his 50th league start for Albion at the expense of Connor Goldson. Defended soundly. **7**

LEWIS DUNK
Mixed bag for the Chelsea fan, who captained the team Bruno's absence. Question marks on both goals but prevented another. **6**

MARKUS SUTTNER
Retained after good performance against Watford. Did okay, although Moses was the biggest threat for Chelsea in the first half. **6**

SOLLY MARCH
Back on the right-hand side and showed signs of striking up a rapport with the galloping Schelotto in the first half. **6**

Chelsea's Michy Batshuayi and Lewis Dunk tangle

DALE STEPHENS
A role in the central midfield three which often meant being faced by Hazard. He gave it a good crack and looked confident on the ball. **7**

DAVY PROPPER
Part of a midfield who had their work cut out combating Chelsea's movement and Kante's knack of winning the ball back. **6**

BERAM KAYAL
Another reminder of the energy he can bring to midfield. Competed well and got a long way forward to turn and shoot over late on. **7**

JOSE IZQUIERDO
Found himself as an auxiliary left-back for much of the time as Chelsea looked to exploit Moses as an attacking outlet. **6**

TOMER HEMED
Retained at the sharp end and had to battle away alone for much of the time. Denied by Cahill when he benefited from decent service. **6**

SUBS
Gross: Offered one reminder of his set-piece accuracy. Murray: Offside when he tested Courtois. Knockaert: Put over a terrific ball which should have brought a goal.

Albion getting

Blues make Seagulls pay from set-pieces

Chelsea	2
Albion	0

ALBION launched the second half of their debut campaign in the Premier League with another tough lesson against one of the elite.

They are now halfway through their fixtures against the 'Big Six'.

Their destiny will be shaped by a dozen of the matches remaining, not the half-dozen against Chelsea, Manchester City, Manchester United, Liverpool, Tottenham and Arsenal.

Their cumulative efforts against the cream have yielded six defeats out of six, four of them by yesterday's margin, with 14 goals conceded and one scored – Glenn Murray's penalty in the home drubbing by Liverpool.

This is not uncommon for established Premier League sides, yet alone newcomers to the division, so it is not a record to be ashamed of.

It just emphasises the gulf between the trophy chasers and the majority of the rest pursuing survival.

Albion, in this respect, remain well-placed in 12th, their cushion over the relegation zone trimmed by a point to four by Bournemouth's last-gasp equaliser against West Ham.

Bournemouth's visit on New Year's Day and, prior to that, the return to Newcastle on Saturday for Chris Hughton to mark the third anniversary of his appointment are the sort of games which will have far more bearing on where they finish.

Hughton has made more changes than usual for the most recent meetings against the giants, Spurs at Wembley and again at Stamford Bridge.

This has been due to the congested schedule and the competitive nature of his squad.

It also makes sense to target matches where his team is far more likely to pick up points.

At the interval there was hope of a breakthrough result.

Antonio Conte's title holders were kept at arm's length by a disciplined display.

There was little to awaken the home supporters, aside from a couple of incursions by Victor Moses, making his 100th Chelsea appearance.

The right wing-back found space down Albion's left flank, patrolled by Markus Suttner and Jose Izquierdo.

Chelsea frontman Alvaro Morata scores their first goal against Albion at Stamford Bridge

Albion goalkeeper Mathew Ryan can do nothing to stop Chelsea scoring their second goal Pic: Simon Dack

By ANDY NAYLOR
Chief sports reporter

Matt Ryan thwarted Moses when Cesc Fabregas picked him out.

On the second occasion the Australian keeper, maintaining his dependable form, was grateful for a header straight into his arms.

Tiemoue Bakayoko could have converted a cross headed back to him by Antonio Rudiger but the ball arrived quickly to the midfielder and it hit him as much as prodding it inches wide.

Apart from that, glimpses of the mercurial Eden Hazard were repelled by Dale Stephens and Beram Kayal, on his second Premier League start, invariably getting a foot in to disrupt Chelsea's predictable domination of possession.

Hughton remarked after Saturday's important home win over Watford that the Seagulls were only halfway through the season's aim.

Similar logic applied to the contest with Conte's team.

No sooner had the second half started than Albion were reminded you cannot switch off for a moment against the best sides. Punishment awaits.

Lewis Dunk lost Alvaro Morata from Cesar Azpilicueta's diagonal cross and the centre-forward, returning from a ban for five bookings, nodded in.

hit for six by elite

Albion defender Lewis Dunk tackles Chelsea midfielder Cesc Fàbregas during the Premier League clash at Stamford Bridge. Pictures: Simon Dack

Chelsea supporters have become accustomed to this combination. It was defender Azpiluceta's sixth assist, all of them for Morata.

That was no consolation to Dunk on a big day for him, captaining Albion in the absence of Bruno against the club he adores.

He has been a tower of strength all season in tandem with Shane Duffy, who was restored in place of Connor Goldson following the Irishman's fleeting suspension.

The Spanish inquisition gathered pace. Marcos Alonso was foiled twice in quick succession by Ryan but not a third time.

The left-wingback, jumping in-between Dunk and Tomer Hemed, met a Fabregas corner on the hour towards the near post with a neatly angled header.

That was that. Dunk cleared off the line from Hazard when Chelsea broke from a corner.

They had 25 shots in total, so it could have been a heavier defeat. Fortunately for Albion, the majority missed the target.

Hughton had an attacking bench in reserve. He would have liked to have used it at 1-0 down or better, not 2-0.

The closest Albion came was in injury time when Duffy headed a free-kick from Pascal Gross, one of those rested, just wide.

Hughton said: "The game generally was not dramatically different to what you'd predict.

"They'd have a lot of possession and ask a lot of questions, and we'd have to defend well.

"The biggest disappointments are the timing of the first goal, which gave them a lift, and the second: conceding from a set-play.

"That's where you think you can be on the same level as them. At 1-0 you're still in the game against a very good Chelsea team, so I'm hugely disappointed with the two goals."

Albion, as Hughton also referenced, need to be better on the ball when they have limited possession to trouble teams.

A pacey attacking outlet in the January transfer window, making opposing defences more wary, would help.

the teams

Albion (4-5-1): Ryan; Schelotto, Duffy, Dunk, Suttner; March, Kayal, Stephens, Propper, Izquierdo; Hemed.
Subs: Gross for Kayal (73), Murray for Hemed (80), Knockaert for March (82) Krul, Bruno, Goldson, Baldock.
Goals: None.
Red cards: None.
Yellow cards: Stephens (57) foul.
Chelsea (3-4-1-2): Courtois; Azpiluceta, Christensen, Rudiger; Moses, Kante, Bakayoko, Alonso; Fabregas; Hazard, Morata. **Subs:** Willian for Hazard (73), Batshuayi for Morata (82), Drinkwater for Kante (85), Caballero, Zappacosta, Ampadu, Pedro.
Goals: Morata (46), Alonso (60).
Red cards: None.
Yellow cards: None.
Referee: Mike Dean (Wirral).
Attendance: 41,568.

stats

ALBION		CHELSEA
1	Shots on	8
7	Shots off	17
1	Corners	13
2	Offsides	1
8	Free-kicks conceded	8
33	Possession	67

Glenn Murray and Gary Cahill

ref watch

Mike Dean earnt howls of derision for a corner award which might not have been as bad a decision as Albion fans claimed. But he showed good sense when the already-booked Stephens fouled just outside the box. **7**

next up

Newcastle United v Albion, Premier League, Saturday, 3pm

and table
Premier League

	P	W	D	L	F	A	Pts
Man City	19	18	1	0	60	12	55
Man Utd	20	13	4	3	43	16	43
Chelsea	20	13	3	4	34	14	42
Liverpool	20	10	8	2	46	23	38
Tottenham	20	11	4	5	39	20	37
Arsenal	19	10	4	5	34	23	34
Burnley	20	9	6	5	18	17	33
Leicester	20	7	6	7	30	30	27
Everton	20	7	6	7	24	30	27
Watford	20	7	4	9	29	35	25
Huddersfield	20	6	5	9	18	32	23
ALBION	20	5	6	9	15	25	21
Stoke	20	5	5	10	23	41	20
Southampton	20	4	7	9	20	30	19
Newcastle	19	5	3	11	19	29	18
Crystal Palace	19	4	6	9	16	29	18
West Ham	20	4	6	10	22	38	18
Bournemouth	20	4	5	11	18	31	17
West Brom	20	2	9	9	14	27	15
Swansea	20	3	4	13	11	31	13

Albion ratings ✓

MATHEW RYAN
Not his busiest game but produced a pair of super saves and was calm on the deck and in the air.
 8/10

BRUNO
Cool and assured on the ball and went forward with adventure in first half. Defended well, notably a first-half header.
 8/10

SHANE DUFFY
An enormous defensive performance against opponents who obligingly tended to look for the aerial route. Might have scored too.
 8/10

LEWIS DUNK
A couple of trademark shot blocks at key times and almost headed the winner when he went up for a second-half set-piece.
 8/10

GAETAN BONG
Recalled to the left-back berth and, after being beaten early on by Hayden, locked things up and looked in charge.
 8/10

ANTHONY KNOCKAERT
Restored to the starting line-up for 150th start in English football. Frenchman worked hard and never stopped wanting the ball.
 7/10

Albion's Shane Duffy impressed in a dominant defensive display

DALE STEPHENS
One or two misplaced passes but composed and controlled in the middle of the park. Refused a shooting chance second half.
 7/10

DAVY PROPPER
Impressive energy and mobility, considering like Stephens he has played every minute of every match.
 7/10

SOLLY MARCH
Had a good battle with Yedlin. Demonstrated his ability to go past players, but final ball was disappointing in promising positions.
 7/10

PASCAL GROSS
Low free-kick from 20 yards, held by Darlow, the only time he threatened to add to his tally. Tireless again in the No.10 role.
 7/10

GLENN MURRAY
Did his best work in the hour he was on retrieving possession. Miskicked with a volley when unmarked, but was offside anyway.
 6/10

SUBS
TOMER HEMED: Diligent and competitive replacement for Murray.

Another point

Shut-out at Magpies is progress for Seagulls

 Newcastle...0
 Albion..........0

ALBION are inching their way towards Premier League safety.

There were more pluses than minuses to be gleaned from an uneventful stalemate at St James' Park.

A halt to the run of four straight away defeats – which included Spurs and Chelsea – represents progress for Chris Hughton on the third anniversary of his appointment and for his players.

Hughton had been beaten on his three previous returns to Newcastle, twice in the Premier League with Norwich and last season with the Seagulls.

His former club also won at the Amex on their way to pipping Albion to the title.

This time around Hughton's side have taken four points off Newcastle following the narrow home victory in September.

The three point gap between them in the bottom half of the table is a fair reflection.

There are more concerns for Rafa Benitez than Hughton, although both are dependent on an effective January transfer window to improve the prospects of survival.

A competitive, low-quality contest for the level revealed nothing about either side that we did not already know.

Both are strong defensively, which has spared them the kind of drubbings encountered more regularly by some of the established Premier League clubs around them.

The problem is in the final third, where they are impotent.

Albion have now gone eight hours and 31 minutes without an away goal since Glenn Murray's winner at Swansea.

The Seagulls were eighth then, which was always going to be flattering. They have only slipped four places, despite one victory in ten matches, which emphasises how many others in the congested scrap to stay up are also struggling for three points.

Newcastle's run is worse, one win in 12. The point was their first at home in six matches and the fifth in which they have drawn a blank.

No prizes for guessing then where the strengthening priority lies for both managers and the respective recruitment teams this month.

St James' Park should be a help

By ANDY NAYLOR
Chief sports reporter

to Newcastle. It becomes a hindrance with a squad of insufficient quality to satisfy the masses.

Albion, enjoying more spells of possession than they have been used to in most away games this season, were the more controlled, composed side.

The Newcastle players seemed inhibited by the desperate need for a home win and the palpable anxiety drifting down from the stands.

The Seagulls could, in fact should, have capitalised on it.

It is ultra-picky to be in any way critical of Shane Duffy and Lewis Dunk. Their primary job is to defend and the central pairing were

outstanding in that respect yet again.

Goalscoring is not their role, but chipping in here and there could be so important to the cause. Both are towers of strength in the air and towering threats inside the opposition box.

Neither of them have made the most of it from set-plays, Albion's likeliest route to goal in recent matches. In the last home game against Watford, for example, Lew-

Albion winger Anthony Knockaert has a powerful shot blocked by the Newcastle defence

Dwight Gayle directs a near post header goalwards but Mathew Ryan made a flying save to deny the striker

Albion defender Lewis Dunk has his goalbound header saved by Karl Darlow
Pictures: Richard Parkes

on road to survival

Newcastle DeAndre Yedlin goes flying in a challenge with Albion winger Solly March

the teams

Albion (4-4-1-1): Ryan; Bruno, Duffy, Dunk, Bong; Knockaert, Stephens, Propper, Gross; Murray.

Subs: Hemed for Murray (62), Kayal, Baldock, Goldson, Izquierdo, Schelotto, Krul.

Goals: None.

Red cards: None.

Yellow cards: Knockaert (73) foul, Dunk (90) foul.

Newcastle (4-4-2): Darlow; Yedlin, Clark, Lascelles, Dummett; Ritchie, Hayden, Merino, Atsu; Joselu, Gayle.

Subs: Perez for Ritchie (72), Shelvey for Merino (76), Murphy for Joselu (84), Diame, Mbemba, Manquillo, Woodman.

Goals: None.

Red cards: None.

Yellow cards: Merino (74) foul.

Referee: Anthony Taylor (Cheshire).

Attendance: 52,209.

stats

ALBION		NEWCASTLE
3	Shots on	2
7	Shots off	9
6	Corners	3
2	Offsides	1
10	Free-kicks conceded	11
55	Possession	45

Mathew Ryan claims a high ball in a solid display

referee

It was not the hardest game but Anthony Taylor had a sound afternoon and rightly waved away penalty claims when Dwight Gayle, booked in midweek for diving, tumbled. **7**

next up

Albion v Bournemouth, Premier League, today (12.30pm).

and table

Premier League

	P	W	D	L	F	A	Pts
Man City	21	19	2	0	61	12	59
Chelsea	21	14	3	4	39	14	45
Man Utd	21	13	5	3	43	16	44
Liverpool	21	11	8	2	48	24	41
Arsenal	21	11	5	5	38	26	38
Tottenham	20	11	4	5	39	20	37
Burnley	21	9	7	5	18	17	34
Leicester	21	7	6	8	31	32	27
Everton	21	7	6	8	25	32	27
Watford	21	7	4	10	30	37	25
Huddersfield	21	6	6	9	18	32	24
ALBION	21	5	7	9	15	25	22
Southampton	21	4	8	9	20	30	20
Bournemouth	21	5	5	11	20	32	20
Stoke	21	5	5	11	23	46	20
Newcastle	21	5	4	12	19	30	19
Crystal Palace	21	4	7	10	18	32	19
West Ham	20	4	6	10	22	38	18
West Brom	21	2	10	9	15	28	16
Swansea	21	4	4	13	13	32	16

is Dunk headed just wide a great chance to double the lead and ease the risk of a slip-up.

This time it was mainly Duffy's turn, back at the ground where he made his Albion debut 17 months ago.

A perpetual danger to Newcastle from Pascal Gross's dead ball deliveries, the Irishman headed over the best of three opportunities from a corner just before the break.

In the second half, another prodi-gious leap from a Gross corner led to Dunk forcing Karl Darlow, deputis-ing for the injured Rob Elliot, into a rare save with a header from close range.

Newcastle only came to life as an attacking force for a fleeting period after half-time. When Albion needed Mathew Ryan the Australian was equal to the task once more.

Ryan is proving to be an excellent acquisition between the posts, agile and pretty secure under the high ball, even though he is not the big-gest of keepers.

He adjusted to keep out a shot by the fit-again Isaac Hayden when wrong-footed by a deflection. Ryan also dived to his left to save a header from the otherwise well-shackled Dwight Gayle from Christian Atsu's cross to secure an eighth clean sheet.

That was as much as Newcastle could muster after Benitez made seven amendments to the line-up which defended deep and doggedly to restrict runaway leaders Man-chester City to a single goal three days earlier.

Hughton reverted to what he would currently regard as just about his strongest line-up with five changes to the side defeated at Chelsea. Another more realistic as-signment against Bournemouth at the Amex today will determine the extent to which Albion have aided their cause over the brutal festive programme.

Cook's header

Set-piece goals hard to swallow for boss

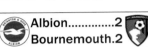
Albion..............2
Bournemouth.2

ALBION'S bad habit of conceding from corners has become as much of an issue as their shyness at the other end of the pitch.

They corrected the latter at the beginning of both halves against Bournemouth with well-worked goals to score two in a game for the first time since the home stalemate with Stoke in November.

The Seagulls courageously came from behind twice that night. This time they led twice, only to be let down by what has turned into a familiar failing of their otherwise resilient identity.

Both Bournemouth equalisers were from corners, the source now either directly or indirectly of five of the last eight goals Albion have let in.

Prior to that it was also the breakthrough route for Liverpool in their emphatic victory at the Amex.

The recurring theme undid all their good attacking work in an end-to-end, entertaining Premier League launch to 2018 containing the most shots (42) of any contest this season.

The first equaliser, by former Seagull Steve Cook in the first half, was the one which really frustrated Chris Hughton.

The Hastings-born central defender rose above Shane Duffy to angle in a looping header.

Albion are not the first team to be hurt by Cook.

He has now scored eight Premier League goals in the last two-and-a-half years.

Crystal Palace's Scott Dann, with nine, is the only central defender who has scored more over that period, but Cook's latest contribution was particularly annoying since Albion had escaped with a severe warning moments earlier when Markus Suttner got a blocking touch to another header from a corner.

The second equaliser by Callum Wilson, 11 minutes from time, was intensely disappointing in terms of the result but less concerning in the way it came about.

Wilson prodded in from close range after a considerable scramble and several rebounds which defied Albion's attempts to clear the danger.

It was an early contender for scruffiest goal of the year – or any year for that matter.

Hughton said of the corner frailties: "You are either going to go zonal or man-for-man.

"We have always gone man for man.

"We have changed some things but ultimately it's about the responsibility of a player of marking somebody.

"He has got to make sure, which ever way it is, he doesn't get a header at goal or certainly a clear header at goal."

Hughton was entitled to feel he would have a happier tale to tell in his 150th match in charge after Anthony Knockaert gave Albion a fifth minute lead, with three clean sheets achieved in the four previous games.

Duffy, Markus Suttner and Pascal Gross were involved in a neat build-up which ended with Jose Izquierdo flashing the ball across the face of goal for Knockaert to convert from a tight angle.

It was not an easy finish for the Frenchman in doubling his tally, having also scored at home against Everton earlier in the season.

Glenn Murray has been going through a lean patch but an opportunity to get the better of the club that discarded him proved inspiring.

A fine, all-round display was rewarded with a sixth goal of the season, which restored Albion's

Albion winger Jose Izquierdo shoots straight at Asmir Begovic as a chance goes begging

Callum Wilson sticks out a leg to level for Bournemouth after a goalmouth scramble

Keeper Mathew Ryan is beaten as Steve Cook steers home a header from a corner.   Pictures: Liz Finlayson

By ANDY NAYLOR
Chief sports reporter

leaves a bitter taste

Albion's Anthony Knockaert, centre, celebrates firing the hosts into an early lead at the Amex against Bournemouth

the teams

Albion (4-4-1-1): Ryan; Schelotto, Duffy, Dunk, Suttner; Knockaert, Stephens, Propper, Izquierdo; Gross; Murray.

Subs: Bruno for Schelotto (76), Brown for Gross (88), Krul, Goldson, Kayal, March, Hemed.

Goals: Knockaert (5), Murray (48).

Red cards: None.

Yellow cards: Propper (81) foul, Murray (89) foul.

Bournemouth (4-4-1-1): Begovic; Smith, Francis, S. Cook, Daniels; Ibe, L. Cook, Arter, Pugh; Afobe; Wilson.

Subs: Ake for Pugh (60), Mousset for Afobe (67), Gosling for Arter (71), Boruc, Simpson, Surman, Butcher.

Goals: S. Cook (33), Wilson (79).

Red cards: None.

Yellow cards: Francis (88) foul.

Referee: Michael Oliver (Northumberland).

Attendance: 30,152 (2,270 away).

stats

ALBION		BOURNEMOUTH
6	Shots on	9
9	Shots off	18
5	Corners	12
1	Offside	0
13	Free-kicks against	9
49	Possession	51

Michael Oliver

ref watch

Michael Oliver made some debated decisions on his third visit this season at the Amex and missed an offside flag leading indirectly to Propper's yellow card. Correct to wave away hopeful Bournemouth penalty appeals. 6

next up

Albion v Crystal Palace, FA Cup third round, Monday (7.45pm).

and table

Premier League

	P	W	D	L	F	A	Pts
Man City	21	19	2	0	61	12	59
Man Utd	22	14	5	3	45	16	47
Chelsea	21	14	3	4	39	14	45
Liverpool	22	12	8	2	50	25	44
Arsenal	21	11	5	5	38	26	38
Tottenham	20	11	4	5	39	20	37
Burnley	22	9	7	6	19	19	34
Leicester	22	8	6	8	34	32	30
Everton	22	7	6	9	25	34	27
Watford	21	7	4	10	30	37	25
Huddersfield	22	6	6	10	18	35	24
ALBION	22	5	8	9	17	27	23
Newcastle	22	6	4	12	20	30	22
Bournemouth	22	5	6	11	22	34	21
Southampton	21	4	8	9	20	30	20
Stoke	22	5	5	12	23	47	20
Crystal Palace	21	4	7	10	18	32	19
West Ham	20	4	6	10	22	38	18
West Brom	21	2	10	9	15	28	16
Swansea	21	4	4	13	13	34	16

Tonight, Premier League: Southampton v Crystal Palace, Swansea City v Tottenham Hotspur, West Ham v West Bromwich Albion, Manchester City v Watford (8.00).

advantage soon after the restart.

Record signing Izquierdo, having comfortably his best game for Albion, was involved again, as was Gross who impressed once more with his intelligence.

Gross's pass released Izquierdo to square for Murray to calmly place his shot past covering defenders on the line.

The adventurous philosophy of Bournemouth manager Eddie Howe ensures they are a side invariably involved in high-scoring games.

The pivotal moment was at 2-1, when Izquierdo raced the length of the field on the counter-attack.

He was through but, with Davy Propper in support, dallied and Asmir Begovic smothered.

Both keepers were busy - it was that sort of match. Shortly before Wilson's equaliser, Jordon Ibe hit a post from 20 yards with a shot which then rebounded off the diving Mathew Ryan and narrowly wide.

Ibe came off the bench to turn the match when the teams met at Bournemouth earlier in the season.

Howe's attacking options, restricted by injuries this time which ruled out Jermain Defoe and Josh King, meant he had a 20-year-old rookie in Matt Butcher on the bench.

That makes the two dropped points for Albion that bit more painful, along with having only one to show for their efforts across the two games against the Cherries, despite leading overall three times.

Together with six home draws, the New Year has begun with a 'what might have been' feeling.

Albion could be well on their way to safety by now, up with Everton and Leicester, instead of still looking a little nervously over their shoulders with one win in 11.

Albion ratings ✓

MATHEW RYAN
Not obviously at fault on the two goals and was out quickly to make a good block from Dawson in the first half. **6**

BRUNO
Stretched defensively in the first half and did not always use the ball well. But did some good stuff in possession and at least hit the target. **6**

SHANE DUFFY
Not at his dominant best against the Baggies front two although he got in a couple of very important headed clearances in the first half. **5**

LEWIS DUNK
Given the slip in some style by Evans for the all-important opener and caused plenty of problems by the Baggies frontmen. **5**

GAETAN BONG
Left exposed to a running jump from Dawson for the second goal. Dawson was often a threat and Bong did not always have enough help. **5**

ANTHONY KNOCKAERT
Gave the ball away cheaply at times in the first half and missed Albion's best chance of the match when they were 2-0 down. **5**

Albion's Bruno acknowledges the fans after the final whistle

DALE STEPHENS
One of the few to emerge with some credit. Read situations well and competed manfully against the pairing of Barry and Krychowiak. **6**

DAVY PROPPER
Plenty of endeavour but not much impact. The workload looks to be catching up with the Dutchman and he was substituted late-on. **5**

JOSE IZQUIERDO
Flattered to deceive with early shot from 20 yards not far off target. No threat or much help to Bong defensively and replaced. **4**

PASCAL GROSS
No repeat of the two-goal heroics at home to West Brom. Looked the one most likely to unlock the door in the first half before fading. **5**

GLENN MURRAY
Lacked service and toiled for little reward against West Brom's strong central defenders. Tad fortunate not to concede a first-half penalty. **5**

SUBS
SOLLY MARCH: Made little impression on the left in place of Izquierdo. **5**
SAM BALDOCK: Perky cameo on Prem debut.
BERAM KAYAL: Competitive but the game was up when he came on.

Survival fight is

Seagulls need help in window to halt slide

  West Brom..2
Albion..........0

CHRIS HUGHTON and his Albion players have done remarkably well to stay out of the Premier League relegation zone since securing their first win at home to West Brom at the start of September.

Four months on, the extra quality of the division is beginning to catch up with them. The aim to stay up is running out of steam.

Only one Albion looked equipped to survive at the Hawthorns. It was not Hughton's team as West Brom ended a run of 20 games without a win with alarming comfort.

The manager and his players need help in what remains of the January transfer window, an injection of attacking quality in the shape of the long sought-after striker and replacement for the stricken Izzy Brown.

Otherwise you fear the worst.

Looking at the remaining fixtures, it is hard to see right now where the points are going to come from to reach the 38 or so which will be required.

Especially if the one glaring defensive weakness – against set-pieces – is not resolved and they continue to look as blunt away from the Amex as they have since Glenn Murray's winner at Swansea early in November.

It is now one win in 12 and no away goal in six-and-two-thirds matches. That is relegation form.

It is no surprise that Albion lost away to Manchester United, Spurs and Chelsea.

This defeat, on the other hand, was as stale as the one last month at Huddersfield, where they also conceded early from a corner.

They have now conceded 17 goals from set-plays, the highest number in the division.

The vast majority have been from corners, a shortcoming transparently spotted and exploited by Alan Pardew.

West Brom forced several early corners and scored from one of them after only four minutes.

The delivery from Matt Phillips was nodded on by Jay Rodriguez for Jonny Evans, sneaking away from Lewis Dunk, to head into the roof of the net.

This fixture had been built up into a must-win for Pardew's side. He appealed for maximum support in the build-up and those dreaded clackers were supplied to help the atmosphere.

Going ahead so early gave the

Craig Dawson climbs highest to head home West Brom's second goal   **Pictures: Richard Parkes**

Albion defender Lewis Dunk heads off target against West Brom

By ANDY NAYLOR
Chief sports reporter

crowd all the encouragement they needed to respond to Pardew's rallying call.

Glenn Murray was fortunate to

escape giving away a penalty when he blocked a fierce shot from Phillips with arms raised to protect his face.

Although not further adrift at the break, it took West Brom just ten minutes into the second half to capitalise again on Albion's defensive Achilles heel.

Dawson met Chris Brunt's corner on the run with a powerful downward header, soaring above

a static Gaetan Bong and defying Anthony Knockaert's attempt at a goal-line clearance.

Albion never really looked like ending the away goal drought, at 1-0 or 2-0 down. An off-colour Knockaert, set up by Murray, sidefooted by far their best chance way over the bar midway through the second half.

Their solitary shot on target was from 25 yards by Bruno, struck

running out of steam

Seagulls winger Solly March is tackled by West Brom defender Jonny Evans in the Premier League loss

Picture: Richard Parkes

the teams

Albion (4-4-1-1): Ryan; Bruno, Duffy, Dunk, Bong; Knockaert, Stephens, Propper, Izquierdo; Gross; Murray.

Subs: March for Izquierdo (46), Baldock for Gross (66), Kayal for Propper (76), Krul, Goldson, Schelotto, Hemed.

Goals: None.

Red cards: None.

Yellow cards: None.

West Brom (4-4-2): Foster; Dawson, Evans, Hegazi, Gibbs; Phillips, Krychowiak, Barry, Brunt; Rodriguez, Rondon.

Subs: Livermore for Rodriguez (79), Nyom for Dawson (81), McAuley for Evans (84), Myhill, Robson-Kanu, Yacob, McClean.

Goals: Evans (4), Dawson (55).

Red cards: None.

Yellow cards: None.

Referee: Martin Atkinson (West Yorkshire).

match stats

ALBION		WEST BROM
1	Shots on	4
12	Shots off	11
6	Corners	9
2	Offsides	3
15	Free-kicks conceded	8
56	Possession	44

referee

Albion were happy with the way Martin Atkinson dealt with the issue involving Gaetan Bong. Waved away penalty appeals against Glenn Murray. **7**

next up

Albion v Chelsea, Premier League, Saturday (12.30pm).

and table

Premier League

	P	W	D	L	F	A	Pts
Man City	23	20	2	1	67	17	62
Man Utd	22	14	5	3	45	16	47
Liverpool	23	13	8	2	54	28	47
Chelsea	23	14	5	4	41	16	47
Tottenham	23	13	5	5	46	21	44
Arsenal	23	11	6	6	41	30	39
Burnley	23	9	7	7	19	20	34
Leicester	23	8	7	8	34	32	31
Everton	23	7	6	10	25	38	27
Watford	23	7	5	11	33	42	26
West Ham	23	6	7	10	29	41	25
Crystal Palace	23	6	7	10	21	33	25
Bournemouth	23	6	6	11	24	35	24
Huddersfield	23	6	6	11	19	39	24
Newcastle	23	6	5	12	21	31	23
ALBION	23	5	8	10	17	29	23
Southampton	23	4	9	10	23	34	21
Stoke	22	5	5	12	23	47	20
West Brom	23	3	10	10	18	30	19
Swansea	23	4	5	14	14	35	17

crisply but straight at Ben Foster.

Supporters complained that Hughton picked the wrong side at Huddersfield. There could be no such protest this time. He selected probably the strongest eleven available to him.

He has problems in both penalty areas at the moment, although the corner goal count can be partly explained by higher quality deliveries, routines, movement and finishing than Albion were accustomed to in the Championship.

Hughton said: "Brunt is probably the best in the country I think at delivering set-plays. That is something that we knew.

"The balance is we are up against better specialists who can generally get the ball where they want to get it but they are still set-plays.

"We have spent season after season having to defend set-plays and the theory of it is no different. So it is hugely disappointing to concede, particularly so early from another set-play.

"The other part of it is we have to be better in that final third. Overall I didn't think there was too much between the two teams.

"I thought we got that ball into the final third with crosses and so forth a good percentage of time, particularly for an away game.

"But of course with no end product. We have to be more productive in that final third and particularly away from home we are finding that difficult."

Three of Albion's next five matches are against sides still below them, including the next two away at Southampton and Stoke.

If results do not pick up over this period then the outlook for survival will be grim.

The**PREM** »

Albion ratings ✓

MATHEW RYAN
Played well again, despite the score. The best of several saves was touching a Willian free-kick on to the post in the second half.
 7

EZEQUIEL SCHELOTTO
Ran his heart out in the right wing-back role, which suits him. Should have been awarded one penalty, if not two, and went close to scoring.
 8

CONNOR GOLDSON
His second Premier League appearance in the defensive re-think. Part of a unit which struggled to cope with Blues' fluid movement.
6

SHANE DUFFY
Rare game to forget. Should have scored with first-half header, hurt in clash of heads, booked and gave the ball away for Hazard's second.
 5

LEWIS DUNK
Captain against the club he adores, with Bruno rested from the formation change. Some good moments defensively and in possession.
6

MARKUS SUTTNER
Preferred to Gaetan Bong but struggled to cope with Moses. Defending not strong enough for the first and fourth goals.
 5

Connor Goldson formed a new-look defensive backline

DALE STEPHENS
Possibly unlucky on the first goal and left chasing Willian's shadow on the second. Mixed fare from then on.
 5

DAVY PROPPER
Went close to his first goal in one of his better performances going forward. But could have done more on both early goals.
 6

PASCAL GROSS
A change of role and he was not a prominent player. But he put over two superb first-half crosses.
 6

SOLLY MARCH
Looked more confident and purposeful than of late and showed good footwork for the first shot on target.
6

TOMER HEMED
The usual graft at the sharp end but needed to make the most of that golden headed to reduce arrears to 2-1.
 5

SUBS
GLENN MURRAY; Sent on for the final quarter just as the chances dried up.
BERAM KAYAL: Did what he could to add midfield energy.
JOSE IZQUIERDO: Got on very late.

Albion fall foul

Run of no points up against big six goes on

 Albion..........0
 Chelsea.......4

CERTAIN elements need to fall into place for Albion to end the relentless run of defeats against the Premier League elite.

They need to defend well, take their chances when they come, have key moments go for them and hope their opponents are a bit below-par.

The absence of each of these requirements made defeat on a heavy scale against the reigning champions inevitable.

Defend well? An advantage was pretty much presented to Chelsea after only four minutes.

Take chances? You hope record signing Jurgen Locadia, watching from the stands, would bury the first-half header Tomer Hemed directed too close to deputy keeper Willy Caballero once the Dutchman shrugs off the hamstring injury accompanying his £14 million capture.

Hemed was not a lone culprit. The missed opportunities for the central defenders to score from set-pieces – rather than Albion conceding from them – continued when Shane Duffy sent a stooping header wide from a corner.

Key moments going in their favour? Not when Jon Moss is the referee.

He denied Ezequiel Schelotto two penalties, one blatant when fellow Argentinian Caballero clearly brought him down, the other less clearcut but still probable when Tiemoue Bakayoko tangled with the rampaging right wing-back.

Davy Propper was also unlucky not to break his duck with a diving header against the upright early in the second half.

In all of these instances the daunting deficit established by falling two goals behind in the opening six minutes would have been halved.

Opponents nowhere near their best? The prospects pre-match were promising. Chelsea, in a barren patch of one goal in four games, were without six mainly first team regulars through injury and suspension.

Of course, they have a depth of quality in the squad which makes them far better equipped to cope with such setbacks.

As it transpired, one of the absentees, far from aiding Albion's cause, disadvantaged them.

Although Alvaro Morata lost Lewis Dunk to head Chelsea into a hard-earned lead at Stamford

Chelsea livewire Eden Hazard rifles home the opening goal early on at the Amex   **Pictures: Simon Dack**

Albion centre-half Shane Duffy is off target with a stooping header against Chelsea

Ezequiel Schelotto has a second penalty shout after a collision with Tiemoue Bakayoko

By ANDY NAYLOR
Chief sports reporter

Bridge on Boxing Day, the Spanish centre-forward has not been in much form.

His two-card dismissal in the FA Cup against Norwich, for a dive then the protest which followed, left Duffy, Chelsea fan Dunk and Connor Goldson – added to the mix in Chris Hughton's reshuffle – facing not a traditional number nine

but a mobile, now you see them now you don't triumvirate of Eden Hazard, Willian and Michy Batshuayi.

It was a hazard too far, as Hughton observed when asked tongue-in-cheek about Chelsea being linked in the transfer market to various tall target men, including Peter Crouch.

"They have wonderful options," he said. "We weren't quite sure what they would do up front but you know they have players in Pedro (also banned), Hazard, Willian that if they are not playing a classic number nine can do wonderful

jobs and be as effective.

"It's a different type of game and in some ways those type of players are more difficult to mark than your classic number nines."

Hazard, with his Messi-type low centre of gravity and slalom shifting of gears, was mesmerising. As painful as the result was for the Amex faithful they will surely have at least derived some measure of pleasure from the chance to witness in the flesh his performance.

He clinically despatched Chelsea's swift breakthrough when Propper initially gave the ball

# of too many hazards

Chelsea goalkeeper Willy Caballero keeps out Tomer Hemed's header and denies Albion a way back into the game at the Amex

the teams

Albion (3-4-2-1): Ryan; Goldson, Duffy, Dunk; Schelotto, Stephens, Propper, Suttner; Gross, March; Hemed.
Subs: Kayal for Gross (68), Murray for Hemed (68), Izquierdo for March (83), Krul, Huenemeier, Rosenior, Baldock.
Goals: None.
Red cards: None.
Yellow cards: Schelotto (17) dissent, Duffy (57) foul, Goldson (79) foul.
Chelsea (3-4-2-1): Caballero; Rudiger, Christensen, Azpilicueta; Moses, Kante, Bakayoko, Alonso; Hazard, Willian; Batshuayi.
Subs: David Luiz for Christensen (57), Zappacosta for Alonso (74), Musonda for Willian (81), Eduardo, Sterling, Ampadu, Barkley.
Goals: Hazard (4), Willian (6), Hazard (77), Moses (89).
Red cards: None.
Yellow cards: None.
Referee: Jonathan Moss (West Yorkshire).
Attendance: 30,600.

match stats

ALBION		CHELSEA
3	Shots on	10
7	Shots off	4
5	Corners	3
2	Offsides	0
12	Free-kicks conceded	5
42	Possession	58

referee

Jonathan Moss could have done with better assistance, be it from the touchline or via a screen. But he had a poor game with the first penalty shout his worst moment. **5**

next game

Middlesbrough v Albion, FA Cup fourth round, Saturday (3pm).

and table

Premier League

	P	W	D	L	F	A	Pts
Man City	24	21	2	1	70	18	65
Man Utd	24	16	5	3	49	16	53
Chelsea	24	15	5	4	45	16	50
Liverpool	23	13	8	2	54	28	47
Tottenham	24	13	6	5	47	22	45
Arsenal	24	12	6	6	45	31	42
Leicester	24	9	7	8	36	32	34
Burnley	24	9	7	8	19	21	34
Everton	24	7	7	10	26	39	28
Watford	24	7	5	12	33	44	26
West Ham	24	6	8	10	30	42	26
Bournemouth	24	6	7	11	25	36	25
Crystal Palace	24	6	7	11	22	37	25
Huddersfield	24	6	6	12	19	41	24
Newcastle	24	6	5	13	22	34	23
ALBION	24	5	8	11	17	33	23
Stoke	24	6	5	13	25	50	23
Southampton	24	4	10	10	24	35	22
West Brom	24	3	11	10	19	31	20
Swansea	23	4	5	14	14	35	17

away and Markus Suttner didn't do enough to stop a cross from Victor Moses which Dale Stephens could, perhaps should, have intercepted.

The second was a blur of one-touch pass and move between the front trio, ended with a flourish by Willian.

Hazard settled matters with 13 minutes left, capitalising on loose play by Duffy with another run which left Albion's backtracking central defensive trio wondering which way to turn before applying another precise finish.

The fourth from Moses with a minute remaining, shrugging off Suttner with ease as he latched onto a sublime pass from young substitute Charly Musonda, ensured Albion were hard done by in much the same way as they were by the 5-1 drubbing by Liverpool.

Their response to the early double blow was admirable. The outcome could not be blamed on Hughton's uncharacteristically dramatic change in tactics and personnel.

Bruno, Gaetan Bong, Anthony Knockaert, Jose Izquierdo and Glenn Murray were all left out. News spread like wildfire that Knockaert's omission from the squad for the second time (after Huddersfield in December) was met with a stroppy exit from the stadium. This was denied by Hughton. The Frenchman, in fact, watched the match from the East Stand. The truth is nobody had genuine cause for complaint about the manager's choices following the diabolical display at West Brom.

Hughton said: "It was mostly because we haven't had too much joy, we haven't scored a goal, against the top six. It was a system to try to match them a little bit, allowed me to play two up front even though Solly (March) played in a little bit of a different way.

"There were decent periods of the game where it worked. What didn't work is they have the quality they have, we made some mistakes and we are finding it difficult to get goals."

Halting Hazard when he is on his game is even harder. "He is a world class player who can produce something out of nothing when you feel you are in good positions," Hughton said.

Albion's Premier League destiny will be determined not by trying to deal with Hazard, Chelsea and company but by matches such as the next four against Southampton, West Ham, Stoke and Swansea.

Spot-on Glenn

Away goal for Seagulls at last in tight draw

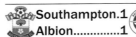

Southampton.1
Albion..............1

THERE is still nothing to choose between Albion and Southampton in the Premier League.

A repeat of the result at the Amex in October, when both teams were in a healthier position in the table, suited the Seagulls more than the Saints, who have now gone 12 games without a win and remain in the relegation zone.

Glenn Murray's early penalty ended the away goal drought for Chris Hughton's side, although they are still the joint lowest scorers in the division with Swansea.

Hughton will hope that Leo Ulloa, introduced as a late substitute on his return to the club, and record signing Jurgen Locadia once he is fit will change that after Jack Stephens earned Southampton a point in the second half.

Former Southampton loanee Dale Stephens was the only starting survivor from Saturday's FA Cup win at Middlesbrough.

Of more relevance were the three changes from the 4-0 home defeat by Chelsea in the Premier League. Gaetan Bong, Jose Izquierdo and Murray came in for Markus Suttner, Connor Goldson and Tomer Hemed as Hughton reverted from the three at the back experiment to his tried and trusted 4-4-1-1 formation.

Skipper Bruno was absent for the third match in succession with a minor back issue which is not expected to sideline him from Saturday's home game against West Ham.

Ulloa, as expected, was on the bench with former Leicester team-mate Anthony Knockaert.

Southampton's adventurous left-back Ryan Bertrand recovered from a hamstring niggle in the FA Cup victory over Watford to take his place in the line-up.

Albion could have gone ahead in the opening minute, Izquierdo blazing over Pascal Gross's cross from 15 yards.

The Colombian should at least have hit the target.

The instant opportunity came during a bright start by the Seagulls which was rewarded by a 14th-minute breakthrough.

Izquierdo and Gross were involved in the build-up as Solly March was clipped down inside the box by the wrong-footed Wesley Hoedt.

Referee Mike Dean, not a friend to Albion in the past, had no hesitation in pointing to the spot.

Murray sent ex-Crystal Palace team-mate Alex McCarthy the wrong way with the penalty, Albion's 200th goal in the top flight and his ninth of the season.

Glenn Murray gets Albion off to a great start with an early penalty at Southampton

Solly March is brought down taking on the Saints defence to win the first-half penalty

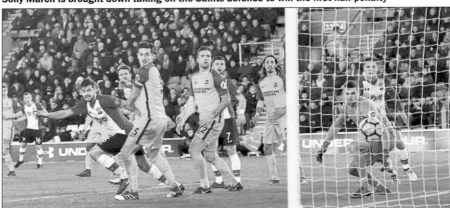
A backheel from Jack Stephens sneaks into a corner for Southampton's leveller   **Pictures: Simon Dack**

By ANDY NAYLOR
Chief sports reporter

It also ended an away goal drought in the Premier League spanning ten hours and 15 minutes since Murray's winner at Swansea in November.

The anxiety among the Southampton supporters was palpable, Swansea's second successive surprise home against Arsenal the night before having dropped them to next-to-bottom.

Mauricio Pellegrino's team tried to respond and began to dominate the ball but Albion held them at bay with relative comfort.

Lewis Dunk produced a fine clearance over his own bar inside the six-yard box to prevent Shane Long converting a cross.

That was the only alarm until a let-off for Mathew Ryan in the 32nd minute. The Australian keeper, taking a touch from a backpass, had his clearance charged down by Pierre-Emile Hojbjerg.

The ball rebounded off the back of the Southampton midfielder as he turned to protect himself and against the bar, with Ryan stranded.

Albion were content to sit back and soak up what Southampton had to offer. March was particularly diligent in his defensive du-

Albion ratings ✓

MATHEW RYAN

Albion fans know how huge penalty saves can be from last year. Ryan plunged brilliantly to his right when the season might have nosedived.

9

EZEQUIEL SCHELOTTO

Not totally at ease in the first half but seemed to defend better in the second period when crosses started flying in.

7

SHANE DUFFY

Helped Albion defend some dangerous crosses and set-pieces. Willingness to get the ball off Ryan was launchpad for the visitors' goal.

8

LEWIS DUNK

A captain's performance. Had already made some soaring interventions from crosses when he produced his goal-saving challenge.

9

GAETAN BONG

His bold overlapping run contributed to the goal as he took right-back Bauer out of the equation. Troubled by Shaqiri after the break.

7

SOLLY MARCH
Preferred to Knockaert, as at Southampton, probably because he is more dependable in defensive duties away from home.

6

Forget a high-five, it was a nine for keeper Mathew Ryan in our ratings

DALE STEPHENS

The best central midfielder on the pitch. Passed it well and involved in the goal. Very unfortunate with the penalty against him.

8

DAVY PROPPER

Excellent for an hour, then lost his way a bit. Couple of good second-half chances spurned to break his duck.

6

JOSE IZQUIERDO

Really beginning to get to grips with the English game now. Tested Butland early, scored another fine goal and contributed off the ball too.

9

PASCAL GROSS

Tidy and good delivery from set-plays. Another assist beckoned with cross for Propper's header chance at 1-0. Withdrawn late on.

7

GLENN MURRAY

Led the line well again. Link up play and ball retention was good. Replaced by Ulloa shortly after Stoke's equaliser.

7

SUBS
LEO ULLOA: No chance to supplement scoring record against Stoke.
BERAM KAYAL: Late warm-up for the Cup.
ANTHONY KNOCKAERT: Vital header off line in late corners flurry.

Late and great

Justice is done after Ryan saves penalty

  Stoke...........1
 Albion..........1

ONCE the dust settles on Albion's debut season in the Premier League, there will be 'if only' moments and matches to reflect upon.

And an almighty great, late escape in the dying stages at Stoke which could well be pinpointed as hugely significant in securing survival.

The bewildering flurry of activity in Albion's penalty area left a stunned Stoke wondering how they had not snatched an undeserved victory and the Seagulls grateful for preserving a point from a performance which warranted all three.

It ranked alongside the unfortunate defeat at Old Trafford as their best of the season away from the Amex.

To have come away with nothing would have been a travesty which would have provoked a different looking bottom half of the table and a different feel in the dressing room than one buoyed by a four-match unbeaten run in all competitions.

Especially as it could have been due to the softest of penalty decisions or, even worse, a final blow of conceding yet again from a corner. That was the fate awaiting Chris Hughton's side when ref Bobby Madley pointed to the spot for a supposed shove on substitute Jese by the outstanding Dale Stephens.

An ensuing squabble between the bitching Spaniard and fellow replacement Charlie Adam over who should take the spot-kick hinted at a disunity alien to Hughton's tight-knit group.

They celebrated in unison when Mathew Ryan dived to his right to keep out Adam's penalty. The lumbering Scot seemed sure to convert the rebound until Lewis Dunk appeared from nowhere behind him with a rescuing challenge.

It did not end there. Ryan was equal to Adam's audacious attempt to score direct from the resulting corner, driven in low to the near post. From the next corner, Mame Diouf's angled header was nodded off the line by Anthony Knockaert, introduced by Hughton just a few minutes earlier.

Albion are entitled to feel justice was done. It was never a penalty, certainly nothing to compare with the blatant one they were denied in the draw between the teams at the Amex earlier in the season, when Ryan Shawcross brought down Glenn Murray. Fortune fa-

Winger Jose Izquierdo finishes off a superb move for Albion to fire them ahead at Stoke City

Albion goalkeeper Mathew Ryan is congratulate after his crucial last-gasp penalty save

Lewis Dunk prevents Charlie Adam scoring in the follow-up from his penalty
Pictures: Richard Parkes

By ANDY NAYLOR
Chief sports reporter

voured them after that, not with Ryan's save but Dunk's last-ditch tackle on Adam and Knockaert's clearance.

Closer scrutiny suggested Dunk's tackle could have resulted in another penalty and a red card. He made more contact with Adam than the ball, which rolled behind

via his hand. Goal-line technology also revealed the ball was halfway across the line from Diouf's header when Knockaert intervened. Staying up or going down threatens to be determined by slender margins, such is the tight and congested nature of the relegation fight.

The breathless chain of events at the finish disguised a cold reality for Stoke. Only they resembled plausible relegation candidates.

Albion, ahead via another wonderful goal from Jose Izquierdo, comfortably had their measure until the richly talented Xherdan

Shaqiri equalised midway through the second half. If the diminutive Swiss winger becomes sidelined, Stoke will almost certainly be done for. The squad assembled by Hughton is less dependent on individuals than the collective, although the inconsistent Izquierdo is certainly flourishing now.

The Colombian troubled Stoke throughout with his pace, directness and finishing power. Shots early on and deep into the second half stung the fingers of Jack Butland along with his sublime breakthrough. First time passing ex-

escape may be vital

Jose Izquierdo is mobbed by Albion team-mates as he rushes to celebrate in front of the travelling Seagulls supporters

the teams

Albion (4-4-1-1): Ryan; Schelotto, Duffy, Dunk, Bong; March, Stephens, Propper, Izquierdo; Gross; Murray.
Subs: Ulloa for Murray (70), Kayal for Gross (79), Knockaert for March (86), Krul, Bruno, Goldson, Locadia.
Goal: Izquierdo (32).
Red cards: None.
Yellow cards: None.
Stoke (4-3-3): Butland; Bauer, Zouma, Shawcross, Pieters; Fletcher, Allen, NDiaye; Shaqiri, Diouf, Choupo-Moting.
Subs: Berahino for Fletcher (46), Jese for Choupo-Moting (62), Adam for NDiaye (79), Grant, Johnson, Cameron, Ramadan.
Goal: Shaqiri (68).
Red cards: None.
Yellow cards: None.
Referee: Bobby Madley (West Yorkshire).
Attendance: 28,876 (3,237).

match stats

ALBION		STOKE
6	Shots on	3
8	Shots off	12
4	Corners	7
2	Offsides	1
10	Free-kicks conceded	6
43	Possession	57

referee

Having waved away two hopeful appeals, it looked like Bobby Madley got it wrong on the penalty but right when he allowed Lewis Dunk's subsequent tackle, despite the defender's own fears. **5**

next up

Albion v Coventry City, FA Cup fifth round, Saturday (3pm).

and table

Premier League

	P	W	D	L	F	A	Pts
Man City	27	23	3	1	79	20	72
Man Utd	27	17	5	5	51	19	56
Liverpool	27	15	9	3	61	31	54
Tottenham	27	15	7	5	52	24	52
Chelsea	26	15	5	6	46	23	50
Arsenal	27	13	6	8	51	36	45
Burnley	27	9	9	9	21	24	36
Leicester	27	9	8	10	39	40	35
Everton	27	9	7	11	32	46	34
Bournemouth	27	8	7	12	31	41	31
Watford	27	8	6	13	37	47	30
West Ham	27	7	9	11	34	46	30
Newcastle	27	7	7	13	25	36	28
ALBION	27	6	10	11	22	36	28
Crystal Palace	27	6	9	12	25	42	27
Swansea	27	7	6	14	20	37	27
Huddersfield	27	7	6	14	23	47	27
Southampton	27	5	11	11	28	40	26
Stoke	27	6	7	14	27	53	25
West Brom	26	3	11	12	21	37	20

changes with Solly March, then the deft-footed Stephens, ripped through Stoke's suspect defences. A well-placed shot beyond Butland for completion, in its own way it was a goal every bit as good, if not better, than Izquierdo's wonder strike in the previous match against West Ham.

The fixture had been billed as Stoke's biggest for a decade, but Albion were so comfortable in the first half there was nothing for the vocal home fans to shout about.

Stoke, short of ideas and ponderous, improved for a change in formation by Paul Lambert, prompted by the half-time withdrawal of the struggling Darren Fletcher and arrival of the goal-shy Saido Berahino.

Albion remained a threat throughout with their crisp counter-attacking. The only flaw in their performance was failing to capitalise on opportunities to either extend or regain the lead. Davy Propper was the guiltiest with a header over from Pascal Gross's inviting cross at 1-0.

Hughton, asked to recall a better away display, said: "Probably this and Manchester United. I thought we were excellent at United, should have got something. It was a deflect-ed goal and the fact it was United, but I thought overall we were very good. We were better than at Swansea and at West Ham (wins) but it's about goals and relieving that little bit of pressure on yourselves."

Amid all the late drama, Ryan's awareness in defying Adam from the corner which followed his penalty save was almost forgotten. Not by Hughton. He said: "There are probably two people that can do that, Charlie meant it. The other one is Shelvey. I think the second one is as good a save, particularly because the emotions at that stage are all over the place."

The final verdict on a crucial quartet of games against fellow strugglers now rests on the result against a resurgent Swansea at the Amex after a likely debut in the FA Cup against Coventry for record signing Jurgen Locadia, an unused substitute in Staffordshire.

A haul of eight points by beating the Swans to conclude the sequence against Southampton, West Ham and Stoke will represent a big step towards safety. Six will be acceptable – depriving others ground gaining victories – five will feel wasteful.

Albion ratings ✓

MATHEW RYAN — 7
Was alert to hold a deflection off Duffy, powerless to save Dunk. But his big moment was that fine save from Ki low to his right at 1-0.

EZEQUIEL SCHELOTTO — 7
The four-man defence does not fully suit his penchant for galloping forays but he was sound and competitive at the back against Swans.

SHANE DUFFY — 7
Could have scored at both ends – with a header against the bar and deflection towards his own net. Would have loved a clean sheet.

LEWIS DUNK — 7
Another crazy deflection to beat Ryan but more significant was his accurate long ball to send Murray away for the penalty.

GAETAN BONG — 7
A good athlete and awkward opponent. Some good moments of defending and looked to get forward.

ANTHONY KNOCKAERT — 8
Justified recall to the Premier League starting line-up in place of March. Took his goal well and contributed with and without the ball.

Dutchman Davy Propper broke forward well for Albion

DALE STEPHENS — 7
Good to see him pop up in the area for assist for Locadia's goal. Wasn't eye-catching but a lot of his best work was unnoticed.

DAVY PROPPER — 7
Dutchman's game has grown. Breaking forward from deep positions more often now, although shooting was wayward.

JOSE IZQUIERDO — 8
Thrived once the game opened up after the break. Played big part in Murray's crucial second and had a hand in Locadia's goal as well.

PASCAL GROSS — 7
Played a bit higher, to intelligent effect, once Swansea's system changed in the second half. Involved in the second and third goals.

GLENN MURRAY — 9
Kane, Sterling and Vardy the only Englishmen ahead of him in the PL goal chart now that he has hit double figures. Fine target man display.

SUBS
SOLLY MARCH: Replaced Knockaert.
JURGEN LOCADIA: Two in two for the record signing.
BERAM KAYAL: Took over from Gross in stoppage time.

Albion coping

Hughton's men stay cool when heat's on

 Albion..........4
 Swansea.....1

ALBION are demonstrating they can deal with the high-pressured environment of the Premier League relegation battle.

The last four matches, away to Southampton and Stoke and at home to West Ham and Swansea, were billed as vital against sides also involved in the fight.

They have emerged from them unbeaten, with eight points and nine goals.

They have also now scored more goals than Burnley and half of the teams below them in the table, accompanied by the best defensive record outside the top seven.

It helps when the heat is on to have unruffled leadership, calmness and consistency.

The contrast between Chris Hughton and Swansea counterpart Carlos Carvalhal in the latest 'six-pointer' for the Seagulls was stark.

The momentum remains with Hughton after their six meetings in the Championship when Carvalhal was in charge of Sheffield Wednesday.

He has now won the last three following the injury-ravaged misfortune of the play-offs two seasons ago.

Carvalhal has revitalised Swansea but he lost the plot as their ten-match undefeated run in all competitions came to an emphatic end.

In the space of half-an-hour either side of the interval, the Portugese used all three substitutions available to him and changed tactics.

It felt like panic and it certainly backfired. Albion's lead provided by Glenn Murray's early penalty was still tenuous when Carvalhal made his third and final change with a quarter of the contest still remaining.

The more attacking players he introduced the more vulnerable Swansea became. Albion raced out of sight with three goals in the last 21 minutes, including two in four minutes soon after Tammy Abraham, the Seagulls' early summer transfer target, became Carvalhal's last throw of the dice.

Carvalhal admitted afterwards he had been reckless. He said bringing on Abraham so early was a "high risk bet" and, with hindsight, he would have left it later.

It is hard to envisage Hughton being so damagingly impulsive. Some supporters still regard him

Albion's Anthony Knockaert scores the third goal

Glenn Murray is felled for his penalty

Pascal Gross shoots

By ANDY NAYLOR
Chief sports reporter

as too cautious.

They were advocating ahead of the match a switch to 4-4-2 and a start for record signing Jurgen Locadia after his debut goal against Coventry in the FA Cup, apparently oblivious to the results and performances against Southampton, West Ham and Stoke.

Hughton's selection and tactics produced Albion's biggest victory in the Premier League and four goals in a game in the top flight for the first time since October 1981, when Manchester City were put to the sword at The Goldstone.

Anthony Knockaert, who scored the third goal, said: "The gaffer said before the game we are going to have to be patient. We won't be able to break them straight away, it's all going to be about being patient and take the opportunity when we get it to break them. And that's what we did, we respected the plan and it worked."

Swansea were obliging participants in turning what promised to be - and indeed proved to be for more than an hour - a nervy afternoon into a romp.

Their charity began when Mike van der Hoorn bundled Murray over from behind. The outcome was the same as at Southampton, Mike Dean pointing to the spot,

with Prem pressure

Anthony Knockaert celebrates scoring Albion's third goal
Pictures: Simon Dack

the teams

Albion (4-4-1-1): Ryan; Schelotto, Duffy, Dunk, Bong; Knockaert, Stephens, Propper, Izquierdo; Gross; Murray.
Subs: March for Knockaert (78), Locadia for Murray (82), Kayal for Gross (90), Krul, Bruno, Goldson, Ulloa.
Goals: Murray (18) and (69), Knockaert (73), Locadia (90).
Red cards: None.
Yellow cards: Murray (63) foul.
Swansea (5-4-1): Fabianski; Naughton, Van der Hoorn, Fernandez, Mawson, Olsson; Dyer, Carroll, Sung-yueng, Clucas; J. Ayew.
Subs: A.Ayew for Dyer (36), Narsingh (der Hoorn 46), Abraham for Carroll (66), Nordfeldt, Routledge, King, Bartley.
Goal: Dunk (85) own goal.
Red cards: None.
Yellow cards: None.
Referee: Mike Dean (Wirral).
Attendance: 30,523.

match stats

ALBION		SWANSEA
5	Shots on	1
11	Shots off	10
3	Corners	5
1	Offsides	0
17	Free-kicks conceded	6
48%	Possession	52%

referee

Mike Dean got the penalty call right and was well advised to rule out a Murray/Knockaert 'goal' for offside. One or two decisions which looked questionable and certainly got the crowd going but he was right to book Murray. **6**

next up

Albion v Arsenal, Premier League, Sunday (1.30pm).

and table

Premier League

	P	W	D	L	F	A	Pts
Man City	27	23	3	1	79	20	72
Man Utd	28	18	5	5	53	20	59
Liverpool	28	16	9	3	65	32	57
Tottenham	28	16	7	5	53	24	55
Chelsea	28	16	5	7	50	25	53
Arsenal	27	13	6	8	51	36	45
Burnley	28	9	10	9	22	25	37
Leicester	28	9	9	10	40	41	36
Everton	28	9	7	12	32	47	34
Watford	28	9	6	13	38	47	33
Bournemouth	28	8	8	12	33	43	32
ALBION	28	7	10	11	26	37	31
West Ham	28	7	9	12	35	50	30
Huddersfield	28	8	6	14	25	48	30
Newcastle	28	7	8	13	27	38	29
Southampton	28	5	12	11	29	41	27
Crystal Palace	28	6	9	13	25	43	27
Swansea	28	7	6	15	21	41	27
Stoke	28	6	8	14	28	54	26
West Brom	28	3	11	14	22	42	20

Murray despatching the penalty.

Murray's determination to hold onto his talisman ranking after the signings of Locadia and Leo Ulloa in January shows no sign of relenting.

He had a second narrowly ruled out for offside and fired just wide before providing crucial breathing space from eight yards after Jose Izquierdo combined with Pascal Gross, Murray's seventh goal in his last nine appearances.

Profiting from the spaces once Carvalhal abandoned the security blanket of three central defenders, which has served Swansea so well during their resurgence, Albion kicked on.

Another well-worked move involving Murray, Pascal Gross and Knockaert was finished off by the Frenchman.

Swansea's late reply, an Abraham drive which Mathew Ryan had covered until it took a violent deflection off Lewis Dunk, was no more than an irritant.

There was still time for Locadia, on for Murray, to mark his Premier League debut with his second goal in as many games from close range, converting a Dale Stephens shot after more incisive wing work by the in-form Izquierdo.

As ever there were moments that might have changed the result. Jordan Ayew struck a post for Swansea at the end of the first half, just after Shane Duffy headed against the bar at the other end.

Ryan also produced a pivotal save early in the second half from a shot by Ki Sung-yueng, Swansea's best player. It was not Albion's most fluent performance of the season but the result is of considerable significance in the context of the survival aim.

Hughton said: "There's no doubt there is a huge benefit getting three pointers, particularly in this division. It's harder for us in the division but at the moment we are in good form and look more likely of that than probably any stage this season."

They are certainly in a good place right now to end their pointless record against the top six when Arsenal visit on Sunday.

Albion ratings ✓

MATHEW RYAN
Aussie exuded more confidence than Cech at the other end. Was busier in the second half, when the highlight was a fine stop from Ozil. **7**

EZEQUIEL SCHELOTTO
Becoming a bit of a favourite. Galloped forward to great effect down the right in the first half. Forced off by collision with Kolasinac. **7**

SHANE DUFFY
Irishman is back towards his dominating best after a mini-blip in the wake of the Republic of Ireland's World Cup agony. Assist for Dunk's goal. **7**

LEWIS DUNK
Gave Albion the early initiative with his first home goal since October 2016. Defended well too, apart from not clearing for Arsenal's reply. **8**

GAETAN BONG
Customary solid contribution and determined defending, especially in the second half when Arsenal dominated possession for spells. **7**

ANTHONY KNOCKAERT
One of his brighter showings, certainly in the first half. Counter-attacks were always going to a key part of the plan and he led a few. **7**

Glenn Murray got top marks for his outstanding leading of the line and goal

DALE STEPHENS
Found it hard to shackle Ozil in one-on-ones but was a part of the collective efforts to make his side hard to be played through. **7**

DAVY PROPPER
Lots of work trying to nick the ball or block passing lanes and made a handful of important contributions to help colleagues. **7**

JOSE IZQUIERDO
Creates excitement but his defensive enthusiasm was occasionally misguided. Went close with a shot cutting inside. **7**

PASCAL GROSS
Curled and arced in a cross which was ideal for Murray to head the winner. Flitted in and out but always has a clever pass up his sleeve. **7**

GLENN MURRAY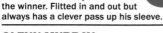
Another goal, another masterclass of centre-forward play for 90 exhausting minutes. Cech error helped him hit the winner. **9**

SUBS
Bruno: Did his bit to maintain the win as Albion saw the job through. **7**
Solly March: Dug in defensively and tried to spark counters.
Beram Kayal: Useful work to run down clock.

Seagulls come

Albion a force to be reckoned with now

 Albion..........2
 Arsenal........1

THIS stirring victory was not just a big six breakthrough for Albion.

It was also their coming of age moment in the Premier League.

An authentic win achieved with a powerful first-half performance and well-managed second half in protecting a lead with few serious alarms.

Against an Arsenal team that will not be that far removed from the one Arsene Wenger sends out in the last 16 of the Europa League away to AC Milan on Thursday evening.

That is the last route to silverware for the Gunners, to salvaging a season that is falling apart.

The respect Albion have now earned from a club with the gravitas of the Gunners was demonstrated by the side Wenger selected.

It showed only three changes to the line-up that made a better fist of trying to compete against Manchester City in the Premier League at the Emirates two-and-a-half days beforehand than at Wembley in the Carabao Cup final the previous Sunday.

Those successive 3-0 defeats will have been draining both physically and emotionally, yet Wenger knew he could not afford to take chances against Albion.

That shows how far they have come since they were comfortably swatted aside at the Emirates in October.

The beleaguered Frenchman was right too. Albion contrastingly showed Arsenal no respect, exploiting their desperate run of form and defensive fragility with ruthless efficiency.

The Seagulls have the worst record in the Premier League for conceding and scoring goals from corners.

It took them only six minutes to improve this aspect of their armoury with a routine manufactured on the training ground by Chris Hughton to expose Arsenal's flimsy zonal marking.

Shane Duffy won an aerial duel with Petr Cech at the far post for Dunk to half-volley in from six yards.

Arsenal were a mess at the back. It could have got worse for them before it actually did, Cech denying Anthony Knockaert.

The second goal duly arrived in the 26th minute. The defending was horrible again, the source and execution familiar by now to Albion supporters.

Gross's inviting cross was headed down and under the hapless Cech by Glenn Murray, rising unmarked between Shkodran Mustafi and Calum Chambers.

Murray's form right now is sensational. Six goals this year is bettered only by Mo Salah and Sergio Aguero.

A rendition of "Murray for England" from the Amex faithful is unlikely to be answered in the affirmative by Gareth Southgate, but he produced another talismanic target man display.

Murray made the most sprints during the match, which raised a chuckle. Released with a free run at goal from deep in the second half, he knew he would not outpace the cover so turned back to rebuild the attack.

There is a cleverness to his play that comes with experience. You do not hold your place in a team of Hughton's for long either if you are not prepared to put in a shift.

By ANDY NAYLOR
Chief sports reporter

Lewis Dunk opens the scoring for Albion

Albion centre-half Lewis Dunk, partly obscured, fires home the opener on the half-volley against Arsenal

Winger Anthony Knockaert is denied a goal by a great save from Arsenal goalkeeper Petr Cech

# of age in Premier

Glenn Murray gets between his Arsenal markers to head home the winning goal for Albion at the Amex.

Pictures: Liz Finlayson and Simon Dack

"We're not the level of team who can afford a striker who stays up front and waits for opportunities," Hughton said. "We need strikers who are prepared to work. That's what he does. He's a player in really good form at the moment, and someone who should get the credit for it."

Albion were a rampant threat in the opening half-hour. They had nine shots, five on target, and have now scored ten times in a hat-trick of home wins in the Premier League, together with another three against Coventry in the FA Cup.

The defending remains generally solid and dependable as well, not more than one goal conceded in a game through an undefeated sequence of seven.

Arsenal's reply just before the interval fell into the soft variety. Dunk failed to clear and Granit Xhaka passed the ball into the box for Pierre-Emerick Aubameyang to flick in from close range.

Laurent Koscielny hit a post with a header soon after as Albion fleetingly wobbled.

They regained their composure throughout the second half, when Arsenal finally upped their game and pressed for an equaliser, although it fell well short of anything resembling an onslaught.

The Gunners were fortunate to finish with 11 on the pitch. Ezequiel Schelotto was flattened by Sead Kolasinac's shoulder in a shuddering collision and Xhaka dived in search of a penalty when Dale Stephens challenged him inside the box. Both had already been booked by replacement referee Stuart Attwell.

Albion did not need help from the officials.

They were too good for Arsenal on their own merits.

the teams

Albion (4-4-1-1): Ryan; Schelotto, Duffy, Dunk, Bong; Knockaert, Stephens, Propper, Izquierdo; Gross; Murray.
Subs: Bruno for Schelotto (69), March for Knockaert (77), Kayal for Gross (86), Krul, Goldson, Ulloa, Locadia.
Goals: Dunk (6), Murray (26).
Red cards: None.
Yellow cards: Stephens (60) foul, Schelotto (64) foul, Murray (79) foul.
Arsenal (4-2-3-1): Cech; Chambers, Mustafi, Koscielny, Kolasinac; Xhaka, Wilshere; Mkhitaryan, Ozil, Iwobi; Aubameyang.
Subs: Welbeck for Iwobi (75), Bellerin for Chambers (83), Nketiah for Iwobi (83), Ospina, Holding, Maitland-Niles, Elneny.
Goals: Aubameyang (43).
Red cards: None.
Yellow cards: Kolasinac (32) dissent, Wilshere (40) foul, Xhaka (54) foul.
Referee: Stuart Attwell (Warwickshire).
Attendance: 30,620 (2,991 away).

match stats

ALBION		ARSENAL
6	Shots on	8
7	Shots off	8
6	Corners	11
5	Offsides	0
13	Free-kicks conceded	12
32%	Possession	68%

referee

Stuart Attwell, replacing Kevin Friend, had a mixed afternoon. Schelotto confirmed he judged the clash with Kolasinac well and he was also right to wave away Xhaka penalty appeals. But there were some strange decisions, not least the yellow card for Stephens. 6

next match

Everton v Albion, Premier League, Saturday (3pm).

and table

Premier League

	P	W	D	L	F	A	Pts
Man City	29	25	3	1	83	20	78
Liverpool	29	17	9	3	67	32	60
Man Utd	28	18	5	5	53	20	59
Tottenham	29	17	7	5	55	24	58
Chelsea	29	16	5	8	50	26	53
Arsenal	29	13	6	10	52	41	45
Burnley	29	10	10	9	24	26	40
Leicester	29	9	10	10	41	42	37
Watford	29	10	6	13	39	47	36
ALBION	29	8	10	11	28	38	34
Everton	29	9	7	13	33	49	34
Bournemouth	29	8	9	12	34	44	33
Swansea	29	8	6	15	25	42	30
West Ham	29	7	9	13	36	54	30
Huddersfield	29	8	6	15	25	50	30
Newcastle	29	7	8	14	27	40	29
Southampton	29	5	13	11	29	41	28
Crystal Palace	28	6	9	13	25	43	27
Stoke	29	6	9	14	28	54	27
West Brom	29	3	11	15	22	43	20

Albion ratings ✓

MATHEW RYAN
Such a shame his fabulous penalty save counted for nothing. Had enjoyed a good match even before that and was sharp to deny Tosun a tap-in.

8

EZEQUIEL SCHELOTTO
A tough afternoon against the dangerous Bolasie. Was especially troubled in the first half. Got forward as Albion chased the game.

6

SHANE DUFFY
The ex-Evertonian looked a bit unlucky to concede the penalty and offered a good showing in front of home fans who applauded him at kick-off.

7

LEWIS DUNK
Had plenty of defending to do and came up with a series of headers and interventions. Could not get close to Tosun as he guided in the second.

8

GAETAN BONG
Among those to do some decent last-ditch stuff in his own box in first half. But was twice caught out by Walcott, the first costing a goal.

6

ANTHONY KNOCKAERT
Loose in possession a couple of times in first half and for Everton's opener. Plenty of endeavour before reckless challenge for red card.

4

Shane Duffy was unlucky to concede a penalty against his former club Everton

BERAM KAYAL
Israeli does not get it easy. Drafted in for his third PL start as Stephens' deputy (others were at Spurs and Chelsea). Lots of grafting.

5

DAVY PROPPER
Break-up of ever-present partnership with Stephens did not unduly perturb Dutchman. Accomplished in most of his work in tricky circumstances.

6

JOSE IZQUIERDO
Coleman and Walcott posed a threat down the left, so Colombian was often occupied with deep tracking to aid Bong. Little going forward.

6

PASCAL GROSS
Albion could not get the influential German into the game and on the ball much at all until match was lost. Dropped into midfield.

6

GLENN MURRAY
Stung Pickford's palms with first-half effort from distance. Little worthwhile service to keep his scoring run going. Taken off at 2-0 down.

6

SUBS
JURGEN LOCADIA: Shot blocked with first touch.
LEO ULLOA: Set up late shot for Gross.
MARKUS SUTTNER: On for injured Bong at full-back.

From a high to

Winger's red caps a bad day at Goodison

 Everton........2
 Albion..........0

THE Premier League can be a fickle mistress. One week the high of beating Arsenal, the next the low of losing at Everton and losing three players, one to a red card and two to injury.

The absences of midfield lynchpin Dale Stephens and left-back Gaetan Bong should thankfully be shortlived.

Anthony Knockaert will have a lot longer to contemplate his recklessness.

Throw in an impotent performance resembling, albeit against stronger opponents, the only other occasions Albion have really let themselves down with corresponding defeats at Huddersfield and West Brom, and Albion's best day against Arsenal was probably followed by their worst at Goodison.

Even so, if you had given Chris Hughton three points from these twin tests before the Gunners fired blanks, he would have shaken your hand (biting it off is not his style).

Results elsewhere ensured that, although Everton have replaced the Seagulls again in the top ten, they still have a healthy cushion over the relegation zone of seven points, which will surely not be reduced to six when Stoke entertain Manchester City tonight.

Everton, dreadful as they have been away, are accustomed to seeing off sides of Albion's calibre at Goodison, where their only defeats have been by top seven occupiers.

Nevertheless, the home witnesses will be wondering how Hughton's side are so far removed from the scrap at the bottom based on a display with little to recommend it apart from customarily sound defence for an hour, led impressively again by Lewis Dunk, and a stunning late penalty stop by Mathew Ryan from Wayne Rooney to avert the heaviest away defeat to date.

There was mitigation to a degree. Losing Stephens to a training ground knock after 46 consecutive league starts, stretching back more than a year to a 3-3 draw at Brentford in the Championship, was a severe blow.

He has become a key figure to such an extent that he had not missed a single minute of action in the Premier League.

Everton's determination to address a decline from ten points out of the first 12 when Sam Allardyce took over to nine from the previ-

Cenk Tosun picks his spot to score Everton's second goal at Goodison Park despite Lewis Dunk's efforts

Albion goalkeeper Mathew Ryan goes full length to his right to save Wayne Rooney's penalty

Mathew Ryan celebrates his penalty save to deny Everton a third goal   **Pictures: Richard Parkes**

By ANDY NAYLOR
Chief sports reporter

ous 33 was evident from the first whistle.

They dominated and yet the crowd were just getting restless when Albion unravelled in the final third of the contest to undo all the solid work inside their own area in the first hour. Everton were pretty much presented with their breakthrough which began with Knockaert, not for the first time, giving the ball away cheaply.

As the ensuing attack developed, Yannick Bolasie was allowed to cut inside to cross to Theo Walcott, sneaking in behind Bong at the far post. The volley into the roof of the net has officially gone down as an own goal. At least the luckless Dunk has company in that respect now. It was the key moment of the

match. Hughton said: "My first impression was it was Walcott's goal. I've been told that it came off Gaetan.

"He (Walcott) was a threat all game, but I felt we dealt with the threat. We knew his running power behind.

"We were against a team with a lot of offensive prowess, but until the goal I was fairly confident we weren't going to concede, so it was a big moment in the game."

Hughton reacted by switching to

a low for Seagulls

Albion striker Glenn Murray climbs above Everton's Phil Jagielka

the teams

Albion (4-4-1-1): Ryan; Schelotto, Duffy, Dunk, Bong; Knockaert, Kayal, Propper, Izquierdo; Gross; Murray.
Subs: Locadia for Kayal (69), Ulloa for Murray (77), Suttner for Bong (81), Krul, Bruno, Goldson, March.
Goals: None.
Red cards: Knockaert (80) violent conduct.
Yellow cards: Schelotto (55) foul.
Everton (4-2-3-1): Pickford; Coleman, Keane, Jagielka, Baines; Rooney, Davies; Walcott, Sigurdsson, Bolasie; Tosun.
Subs: Calvert-Lewin for Walcott (73), Holgate for Bolasie (78), Klaassen for Davies (84), Robles, Martina, Niasse, Baningime.
Goals: Bong OG (60), Tosun (76).
Red cards: None.
Yellow cards: None.
Referee: Roger East (Wiltshire).
Attendance: 39,199.

match stats

ALBION		EVERTON
4	Shots on	6
3	Shots off	10
3	Corners	10
1	Offsides	2
14	Free-kicks conceded	10
41	Possession	59

referee

Anthony Knockaert gave Roger East an easy decision as Albion received their first red card of the season. He was right to book Schelotto too but the penalty looked debatable. **7**

next up

Manchester United v Albion, FA Cup quarter-finals, Saturday (7.45pm).

and table

Premier League

	P	W	D	L	F	A	Pts
Man City	29	25	3	1	83	20	78
Man Utd	30	20	5	5	58	23	65
Tottenham	30	18	7	5	59	25	61
Liverpool	30	17	9	4	68	34	60
Chelsea	30	17	5	8	52	27	56
Arsenal	30	14	6	10	55	41	48
Burnley	30	11	10	9	27	26	43
Leicester	30	10	10	10	45	43	40
Everton	30	10	7	13	35	49	37
Watford	30	10	6	14	39	50	36
ALBION	30	8	10	12	28	40	34
Bournemouth	30	8	9	13	35	48	33
Newcastle	30	8	8	14	30	40	32
Swansea	30	8	7	15	25	42	31
Huddersfield	30	8	7	15	25	50	31
West Ham	30	7	9	14	36	57	30
Southampton	30	5	13	12	29	44	28
Crystal Palace	30	6	9	15	28	48	27
Stoke	29	6	9	14	28	54	27
West Brom	30	3	11	16	23	47	20

4-4-2, introducing Jurgen Locadia for Stephens' replacement Beram Kayal and dropping Pascal Gross deeper, but the tone had been set. Albion's passing on the counter throughout let them down and the response was muted.

Cenk Tosun, Everton's £27 million signing from Besiktas in January, sealed their fate, firing in his second goal as many games via the underside of bar after an exchange of passes with Leighton Baines.

Everton's first clean sheet of the year was only seriously threatened by an audacious effort by Gross straight from the restart, which was just too high.

Knockaert's dismissal, following his post-substituted strop against Arsenal, was senseless, a two-footed jump tackle close to the touchline which bemused the evading Baines.

Early in the season at Watford, Knockaert was the victim of a similar but worse tackle by Miguel Britos, who ran further and caught him on the knee rather than, as in this instance, on the ankle.

It was, nevertheless, indefensible. Knockaert will now pay a heavy price for his volatile temperament, missing the FA Cup quarter-final at Manchester United and the vital home games back-to-back against his old club Leicester and Huddersfield.

If Solly March grasps the opportunity, Knockaert's inactivity could last even longer than five weeks.

Bong departed with his right thigh strapped. Unfortunately for Ryan, unlike his stoppage time denial of Charlie Adam from the spot at Stoke, the agile Australian's brilliance in foiling Rooney's crisply struck penalty was immaterial to the result.

It was given away by Shane Duffy, bringing down substitute Dominic Calvert-Lewin, a blemish on the Irishman's return to his first club.

Heavier punishment awaits if Albion's performance, particularly in possession, is as lacklustre at Old Trafford.

Albion ratings ✓

MATHEW RYAN
Not really involved. Was comfortable on either foot and held routine low efforts from Vardy and Mahrez before twice being left powerless. **6**

EZEQUIEL SCHELOTTO
Defended pretty well bar a very late switch-off which didn't matter for the second goal. Can do more than this going forward. **7**

SHANE DUFFY
Plenty of decent defending against Vardy before going forward for the final push. Presence played a part in Ndidi's dismissal. **7**

LEWIS DUNK
A comfortable afternoon defensively as Vardy lived off scraps – right up until that final attack. Looks comfortable on the ball. **7**

GAETAN BONG
Defended well against Mahrez, who was only an influence after going infield. But high mark reduced for lack of marking for Iborra goal. **7**

JURGEN LOCADIA
Mobile liverwire in first half on his full Premier League debut, right, centre and left. Less of an influence second half and eventually replaced. **7**

Jurgen Locadia had a roaming role on his full Premier League debut

BERAM KAYAL
First home Premier League start coincided with 100th appearance for the club. Marked them both with a strong and energetic performance. **7**

DAVY PROPPER
Assumed the role of composed, midfield marshal compently in the absence of Stephens after busy international 'break' with the Dutch. **7**

JOSE IZQUIERDO
A threat once Albion got him more involved in the second half. Won the penalty and worried Leicester when the ball was at his feet. **7**

PASCAL GROSS
Accomplished again. Almost added to assists and goals tallies with pass for Murray's first-half chance and a shot after the break. **7**

GLENN MURRAY
Not his day at the Amex this time. Missed the target with first-half chance, hit it with penalty, but Schmeichel guessed right. **5**

SUBS
SOLLY MARCH: Instant impact by helping win spot-kick.
SAM BALDOCK: Brief home Premier League debut at 0-1.

It's the one that

Seagulls' home form should be even better

 Albion..........0
 Leicester.....2

ALBION'S form at the Amex in the Premier League has been impressive.

It has produced 24 of their 34 points and is good enough for a place in the top eight. But it should be even better.

Draws that should have been wins earlier in the season, against the likes of Everton and Bournemouth, had almost been forgotten after three straight home victories in the top flight for only the third time in the club's history.

Now a defeat that should have been a win can be added to the 'if only' tally.

The singular similarity to the first clash with Leicester was the identical scoreline, a horrible anomaly.

Albion looked every inch Premier League novices in the East Midlands in their opening away game back in August.

They looked every inch a bona fide Premier League this time. You get what you deserve over the course of 38 games but Chris Hughton's side did not get what they deserved in the 31st.

They would have without a rare off day in front of goal on home soil for Glenn Murray.

He has scored 36 goals in 79 games since returning from Bournemouth 20 months ago. Twenty-seven of them have been at the Amex, including six in six prior to this aberration.

Murray will be glad to see the back of Leicester. An ankle injury sustained at the King Power Stadium hampered him in the early stages of the season.

Kasper Schmeichel outFoxed him when the opportunity presented itself to reward Albion's superiority deep into the second half.

Jose Izquierdo was sandwiched by Wilfred Ndidi and Harry Maguire. Murray checked his run-up in an attempt get the better of Schmeichel from the ensuing penalty. The Danish keeper was not fooled, guessed correctly and dived to his left to save the spot-kick, struck at a convenient height.

Murray and Schmeichel have both been around long enough to appreciate their occupational hazards. Goalscorers and goalsavers can be heroes one minute, villains the next.

Schmeichel was the latter in Leicester's previous match prior to the international break, beaten by Pedro to a cross for Chelsea's extra-time winner in the quarter-finals of the FA Cup.

It was Murray's turn to be in the dock, not just for the penalty but a glaring first-half miss of the target, also from 12-yard range,

A late chance goes begging for Albion

Glenn Murray's penalty is saved by Kasper Schmeichel

Wilfred Ndidi writhes in frustration as he sees red while Shane Duffy writhes in pain

By ANDY NAYLOR
Chief sports reporter

when Pascal Gross's pass put him through and Schmeichel was off his line sharply to close him down.

While Murray probably cost Albion three points, he has won them many more with his goals, including four successful penalties.

Hughton said: "It's no different if a defender makes a mistake which leads to a goal. We don't generally question too much, we make decisions and hope they are the right ones. Glenn this season has been very good – look at the goals he's scored. He's scored goals that have won us games. Even in a hugely disappointing moment, these are the things you still have to remember."

It should be remembered as well, continuing the swings and roundabouts theme, how much more uncomfortable the bottom of the table would look had it not been for Matthew Ryan's last-gasp penalty save at Stoke a few weeks ago.

got away for Albion

Jose Izquierdo goes down for Albion's penalty at the Amex
Pictures: Simon Dack and Liz Finlayson

the teams

Albion (4-4-1-1): Ryan; Schelotto, Duffy, Dunk, Bong; Locadia, Kayal, Propper, Izquierdo; Gross; Murray.
Subs: March for Locadia (75), Baldock for Kayal (84), Krul, Bruno, Goldson, Suttner, Hemed.
Goals: None.
Red cards: None.
Yellow cards: Kayal (66) foul, Bong (79) foul.

Leicester (4-4-1-1): Schmeichel; Simpson, Morgan, Maguire, Chilwell; Mahrez, Ndidi, Iborra, Albrighton; Okazaki; Vardy.
Subs: Diabate for Okazaki (56), Gray for Albrighton (79), Fuchs for Mahrez (85), Jakupovic, Iheanacho, Silva, Dragovic.
Goals: Iborra (83), Vardy (90).
Red cards: Ndidi (24) foul and (87) foul.
Yellow cards: Morgan (12) foul, Chilwell (63) foul, Simpson (64) foul, Maguire (68) foul.
Referee: Chris Kavanagh (Lancashire).
Attendance: 30,629.

match stats

ALBION		LEICESTER
3	Shots on	4
12	Shots off	2
6	Corners	1
6	Offsides	1
11	Free-kicks conceded	13
47%	Possesion	53%

referee

Chris Kavanagh gave out plenty of cards but had a good game with the one major question mark over Ndidi's second yellow. Should probably have booked Schmeichel for his penalty protest which might have hurried the Foxes keeper up in the final stages. **7**

next match

Albion v Huddersfield, Premier League, Saturday (3pm).

and table

Premier League

	P	W	D	L	F	A	Pts
Man City	31	27	3	1	88	21	84
Man Utd	31	21	5	5	60	23	68
Liverpool	32	19	9	4	75	35	66
Tottenham	31	19	7	5	62	26	64
Chelsea	31	17	5	9	53	30	56
Arsenal	31	15	6	10	58	41	51
Burnley	31	12	10	9	29	27	46
Leicester	31	11	10	10	47	43	43
Everton	32	11	7	14	38	53	40
Bournemouth	32	9	10	13	39	51	37
Watford	32	10	7	15	41	57	37
Newcastle	31	9	8	14	31	40	35
ALBION	31	8	10	13	28	42	34
West Ham	31	8	9	14	39	57	33
Swansea	31	8	7	16	25	44	31
Huddersfield	32	8	7	17	25	53	31
Crystal Palace	32	7	9	16	31	50	30
Southampton	31	5	13	13	29	47	28
Stoke	32	6	9	17	29	61	27
West Brom	32	3	11	18	25	51	20

Albion were still on course for a point and first clean sheet of 2018 against a lacklustre Leicester until lanky midfielder Vicente Iborra headed in Ben Chilwell's left-wing cross seven minutes from time.

A flattering lead was doubled in stoppage time with a tap-in for an otherwise subdued Jamie Vardy, his tenth goal in his last 12 starts for club and country, from sub Demarai Gray's cross, with Shane Duffy left upfield in a desperate attempt to salvage parity.

Leicester had been reduced to ten men by then. The inconsolable Ndidi, booked in the first half for an obvious foul on Beram Kayal, was a little unfortunate to be cautioned again when Duffy strode forward and made a meal of a more innocuous challenge.

Leicester will qualify for the Europa League if they finish seventh, in the likely event of Southampton not winning the FA Cup.

Escaping from the bottom three is a much bigger priority for Saints, one of several still well adrift of Albion with time running out.

Defeat, although hard to take, did not do too much damage and there was plenty to like about the performance, not least in stifling the menace of Vardy and Riyad Mahrez.

Record signing Jurgen Locadia made an encouraging full Premier League debut, Beram Kayal's display disguised the continuing absence of the hamstrung Dale Stephens and Gross was economically influential again.

Hughton said: "At the moment it hurts and it will for the next couple of days. But what they (players) will be lifted by is another opportunity at home next Saturday. It's a big opportunity for us."

Indeed it is against fast-falling Huddersfield. The state of play still looks a lot healthier for Albion than them.

Albion ratings ✓

MATHEW RYAN
Nothing he could do about the goal. Did everything asked of him otherwise shot-saving and handling – which was not a great deal. **7**

EZEQUIEL SCHELOTTO
Part of general looseness in possession at the back at times. Handled van La Parra pretty well and tested Lossl with second-half shot. **6**

SHANE DUFFY
Rare off day for the big Irishman. Gifted the equaliser, missed a good chance and risked a second yellow for foul on van La Parra. **5**

LEWIS DUNK
Not at his best with the ball but was still solid. Had a great chance with close range header from a corner in the second half. **6**

GAETAN BONG
Had the better of Ince. Sound and strong defensively, especially on the floor inside his own penalty area. **7**

SOLLY MARCH
Could not lay claim to Albion's first goal in four games but was quite bright down the right and helped Albion revert to more well-balanced shape. **6**

Jose Izquierdo missed a good chance when put through as a heavy touch let him down

DALE STEPHENS
A welcome return from injury and he did OK without imposing himself on proceedings. Denied by Lossl with a 20-yard effort. **6**

DAVY PROPPER
Did a lot of good stuff, notably a fine through pass for Izquierdo, but afternoon was tarnished by early miss and the red card. **5**

JOSE IZQUIERDO
Frustrating. Is always threat, always busy and his decision-making was better but too often let down with poor execution or heavy touch. **5**

PASCAL GROSS
A quiet game for the man who might have been looked upon as a game-changer. Involved in a nice second half-move but taken off. **6**

GLENN MURRAY
Sent a tough header off target in first half and played a clever return pass to send Izquierdo clear. Link-up play dropped below normal level. **6**

SUBS
Leo Ulloa: Produced some nice touches at close quarters, notably to send Izquierdo clear.
Beram Kayal: Sent on to replace Propper in midfield after red card.

Albion have an

Seagulls blow big chance for a vital win

Albion............1
Huddersfield.1

ALBION probably do not need to win another game to stay up.

That is just as well after blowing their best chance to take three more points.

This was the stand-out opportunity in their remaining matches, especially after going ahead.

Huddersfield, struggling for form and goals, have been hopeless at playing catch-up in the Premier League.

They had lost 16 times out of 17 after conceding the opening goal but Albion gifted them only their second point from a losing position.

The Seagulls are crawling towards safety the only way they know how - the hard way.

One point from successive home games against Leicester and Huddersfield was not the return Chris Hughton hoped for to compensate for such a challenging run-in.

Hughton summed it up. He said: "We played well last week, didn't win, didn't play as well this week but had better chances to win it."

Huddersfield, spurred on by former Albion transfer targets Alex Pritchard and Aaron Mooy, deserved their point on the balance of play.

Based on chances, Albion should have won with something to spare.

Against Leicester, Glenn Murray missed a sitter and had a penalty saved. This time two sitters were squandered, together with two other golden opportunities to improve on a wretched scoring record from set-pieces.

Add to that a gift-wrapped equaliser and a below-par performance should nevertheless have produced a victory to ease the palpable anxiety which engulfed the Amex.

Hughton said: "Everybody knows how important a win is and the points it puts us on. Some think it would be close to giving us enough.

"All of that's normal. Whether some of that seeps through to the players I don't know, but it certainly wasn't one of our better performances."

Two of the most dependable players in the spine of the side over the course of the campaign typified the general malaise.

Huddersfield's high press and high defensive line backfired inside the opening minute but Davy Propper fired wide when clean through.

The Dutch midfielder has yet to transfer his scoring touch with

By ANDY NAYLOR
Chief sports reporter

former club PSV Eindhoven and at international level, although in fairness he generally occupies a deeper role.

His effective partnership with

Jose Izquierdo shoots straight at Huddersfield keeper Jonas Lossl when through
Pictures: Liz Finlayson

Steve Mounie rounds Mathew Ryan to score the equaliser after Shane Duffy's poor pass gifted him the ball

Solly March and Dale Stephens celebrate after Lossl allows his low strike to creep in, right, for an own goal

Dale Stephens, reunited by the latter's return from hamstring trouble, could be instantly broken up again for half of the six fixtures remaining after Propper was sent-off 15 minutes from time for a tackle on Jonathan Hogg.

Referee Anthony Taylor dismissed the already-booked Victor Moses for a blatant dive in last season's FA Cup final.

Propper's punishment was more contentious. It was a strong challenge but not a high one, worthy of a yellow or perhaps an appropriate orange if such a punishment existed.

There is sufficient doubt for Albion to surely mount a nothing-to-lose appeal, because it would not fall into the frivolous category which risks an even stiffer sentence.

Hughton said: "I don't think the

off day at the Amex

Davy Propper shows his frustration after missing a clear chance in the opening minutes of the match against Huddersfield

the teams

Albion (4-4-1-1): Ryan; Schelotto, Duffy, Dunk, Bong; March, Stephens, Propper, Izquierdo; Gross; Murray.
Subs: Ulloa for Murray (67), Kayal for Gross (76), Krul, Bruno, Goldson, Locadia, Baldock.
Goal: Lossl (29) own goal.
Red card: Propper (75) serious foul play.
Yellow card: Duffy (59) foul.
Huddersfield (4-4-1-1): Lossl; Hadergjonaj, Jorgensen, Schindler, Kongolo; Ince, Hogg, Mooy, Van La Parra; Pritchard; Mounie.
Subs: Billing for Hogg (80), Quaner for van La Parra (89), Coleman, Smith, Malone, Lowe, Depoitre.
Goals: Mounie (33).
Red cards: None.
Yellow cards: None.
Referee: Anthony Taylor (Cheshire).
Attendance: 30,501.

match stats

ALBION		HUDDERSFIELD
4	Shots on	5
9	Shots off	9
5	Corners	3
3	Offsides	3
13	Free-kicks	7
41%	Possession	59%

referee

Anthony Taylor made a questionable call to dismiss Davy Propper, possibly on someone's advice. Did well to resist calls for what would have been a second yellow against Shane Duffy. **6**

next up

Crystal Palace v Albion, Premier League, Saturday (3pm).

and table

Premier League

	P	W	D	L	F	A	Pts
Man City	32	27	3	2	90	24	84
Man Utd	32	22	5	5	63	25	71
Liverpool	33	19	10	4	75	35	67
Tottenham	32	20	7	5	64	27	67
Chelsea	32	17	6	9	54	31	57
Arsenal	32	16	6	10	61	43	54
Burnley	32	13	10	9	31	28	49
Leicester	32	11	10	11	48	45	43
Everton	33	11	8	14	38	53	41
Newcastle	32	10	8	14	33	41	38
Bournemouth	33	9	11	13	41	53	38
Watford	33	10	7	16	42	59	37
ALBION	32	8	11	13	29	43	35
West Ham	32	8	10	14	40	58	34
Swansea	32	8	8	16	26	45	32
Huddersfield	33	8	8	17	26	54	32
Crystal Palace	33	7	10	16	33	52	31
Southampton	32	5	13	14	31	50	28
Stoke	33	6	9	18	30	63	27
West Brom	33	3	12	18	26	52	21

referee is in a good enough position to assess it properly, so taking that into consideration I think it's harsh. If you give red cards for that you will see a whole heap more week in, week out."

Propper's misery was matched by Shane Duffy after Jonas Lossl allowed a low drive from the recalled Solly March to creep in via a diving deflection onto the post and then rebound off the poorly positioned keeper.

Duffy did not look with a backpass which Steve Mounie intercepted to round Mathew Ryan and convert his third goal of the season against Albion.

The normally reliable Irish central defender, fortunate not to receive a second caution from Taylor for a foul on Rajiv van La Parra, capped an uncharacteristic display with a header off target from a cor-ner which ought to have been buried once Propper had been dismissed.

Duffy's accomplice Lewis Dunk headed across the face of goal, instead of into it, from three yards from another corner. Then, again with ten men, Jose Izquierdo's dallying and poor touch when substitute Leo Ulloa sent him clear enabled Lossl to smother the Colombian.

Hughton said: "They are the moments. Down to ten men, Jose scores that goal, we come away with a huge sigh of relief. I would say it was a game we deserved to win, simply because of chances, maybe not on the balance of play but on chances."

Huddersfield have a hard finish as well and are still three points behind Albion with a worse goal difference. Guaranteed survival remains tantalisingly close and Selhurst Park would be a satisfying stage on which to extinguish any lingering doubts.

Albion ratings ✓

MATHEW RYAN
Looked uneasy on the second goal and could he have come for the third? But a sharp save kept Albion in it and a spectator in second half.
5

EZEQUIEL SCHELOTTO
Given a torrid time on the ground by an on-song Zaha, which can happen. But in the air as well? Improved a little in the second half.
5

SHANE DUFFY
Part of a back-line which looked hopelessly out of sorts in that costly first-half. Rumbled forward late on to no avail.
6

LEWIS DUNK
Strong work and a soaring header set up Albion's first goal but was outmanoeuvred by Tomkins for the first header on the Palace goal.
6

GAETAN BONG
Maybe the best of the back-line, which is not saying too much, and acted as a stand-in winger before the real thing was sent on in March.
6

JOSE IZQUIERDO
Lovely finish once he was on his preferred left flank, cutting onto that lethal right foot, to join Gross on five goals.
7

Albion winger Jose Izquierdo produced a superb finish for his goal

PASCAL GROSS
Is less effective deeper on the right than in the No.10 role, although understandable Hughton took that route with Propper suspended.
6

DALE STEPHENS
Early booking for clattering Zaha left him vulnerable to another from Andre Marriner. Tested Hennessey from long range in the second half.
6

BERAM KAYAL
Did not let the side down, deputising for Propper. Crossed for both of Murray's second-half chances. Late caution for upending Zaha.
7

JURGEN LOCADIA
Record signing is still finding his feet. Combined with Izquierdo for the Colombian's goal but found wanting at times without the ball.
5

GLENN MURRAY
In the right place to halve the arrears and unlucky with second-half volley, but late one misdirected should have denied old club the points.
6

SUBS
ANTHONY KNOCKAERT 6: Part of second-half improvement.
LEO ULLOA: Flick-on for Murray's late chance.
SOLLY MARCH: Few minutes as a left wing-back.

Seagulls press

Albion gift soft goals in defeat to arch rivals

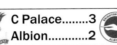
C Palace........3
Albion............2

MERCI Olivier Giroud.

The fight to stay out of the bottom three would look a whole lot more worrying for Albion without the two-goal Frenchman inspiring Chelsea's comeback at Southampton.

It is customary for sides managed by Mark Hughes this season to leak three goals or more. First Stoke, now Saints.

The same cannot usually be said of teams in the care of Chris Hughton. Provided with the comfort of Chelsea's recovery on the south coast in the early kick-off, Albion proceeded to wreck their chances of sealing safety with catastrophic defending.

It took them just 24 minutes to concede three goals in an away game for the first time in the Premier League.

What a time to press self-destruct and keep the finger on the button, against the old enemy in even greater need of the points themselves.

Looking on the bright side, Albion managed in the first half to equal their tally of goals in their previous nine away league outings against Palace's ropey rearguard.

There is nothing wrong with the spirit either. A strong second-half display should have produced a point.

But unless Albion stop letting in soft goals at one end and start taking more of their chances at the other, Hughton's plea to his players to achieve survival on their own merits, rather than depending on the inadequacies of others, will fall on deaf ears.

The goal difference will take a mighty hammering if they defend like this against Spurs, Burnley, Manchester United, Manchester City and Chelsea.

Instead of silencing Palace's notoriously noisy support at Selhurst Park, the home fans were bouncing with a mixture of joy and disbelief at the benevolence of their 'neighbours'.

Palace did not have to work at all for any of their goals. The ease with which they were presented with their early breakthrough was staggering.

When Luka Milivojevic worked a routine short corner with Ruben Loftus-Cheek, they had only Jurgen Locadia for company.

Why Dale Stephens or somebody else did not react sooner and vacate the area to assist the outnumbered Dutchman was bemusing.

Striker Glenn Murray gets on the end of a cross late on but volleys wide rather than in from close range

Defender Lewis Dunk outjumps his marker to head goalwards and set up Glenn Murray's goal

Jose Izquierdo finishes superbly for Albion's second goal

By ANDY NAYLOR
Chief sports reporter

Milivojevic drove low across the face of goal, Mathew Ryan stretched out an unconvincing hand and Wilfried Zaha tapped in at the far post just before the ball crossed the line.

Palace's second was a tale of similar collective incompetence, a reminder of that period when it felt as if Albion were conceding from corners in every game.

This one initially found the head of James Tomkins, with Ezequiel Schelotto statuesque. Ryan, unsighted, got a hand to it and the second decisive effort from Tomkins after Shane Duffy had blocked James McArthur's initial follow-up.

The Australian keeper, so de-pendable normally, did not cover himself in glory, but the chaotic defending around him offered little protection. Zaha was Albion's nemesis again after knocking them out of the Championship play-offs at the Amex five years ago with two goals.

His second was a collector's item. Milivojevic had all the time in the world to pick him out.

He ran off the back of Schelotto to head in at the far post, a first with that part of his anatomy in

self-destruct button

A pair of Eagles players get above Seagulls' Glenn Murray
Pictures: Simon Dack

the teams

Albion (4-3-3): Ryan; Schelotto, Duffy, Dunk, Bong; Gross, Stephens, Kayal; Izquierdo, Murray, Locadia.
Subs: Knockaert for Locadia (46), Ulloa for Gross (70), March for Bong (85), Krul, Bruno, Goldson, Baldock.
Goals: Murray (18), Izquierdo (34).
Red cards: None.
Yellow cards: Stephens (11) foul, Kayal (90) foul.
Palace (4-4-2): Hennessey, Ward, Sakho, Tomkins, van Aanholt; McArthur, Cabaye, Milivojevic, Loftus-Cheek; Zaha, Townsend.
Subs: Benteke for Cabaye (69), Riedewald for Loftus-Cheek (77), Speroni, Sarloth, Lee, Bissaka, Kelly.
Goals: Zaha (5), Tomkins (14), Zaha (24).
Red cards: None.
Yellow cards: Milivojevic (16) handball, Zaha (76) dissent,

stats

ALBION		CRYSTAL PALACE
3	Shots on	9
8	Shots off	7
6	Corners	5
1	Offsides	2
16	Free-kicks conceded	12
50%	Possession	50%

Dale Stephens fights for the ball with Joel Ward, left

referee

Andre Marriner is not card happy and that style suited this torrid tussle. Resisted calls to show second yellows to Stephens and Milivojevic. Well assisted on Albion's second goal as Izquierdo was correctly deemed onside. **8**

next up

Albion v Spurs, Premier League, tomorrow (7.45pm).

and table

Premier League

	P	W	D	L	F	A	Pts
Man City (C)	33	28	3	2	93	25	87
Man Utd	33	22	5	6	63	26	71
Liverpool	34	20	10	4	78	35	70
Tottenham	33	20	7	6	65	30	67
Chelsea	33	18	6	9	57	33	60
Arsenal	33	16	6	11	62	45	54
Burnley	33	14	10	9	33	29	52
Leicester	33	11	10	12	49	47	43
Everton	34	11	9	14	39	54	42
Newcastle	33	11	8	14	35	42	41
Bournemouth	34	9	11	14	41	56	38
Watford	34	10	7	17	42	60	37
ALBION	33	8	11	14	31	46	35
Huddersfield	34	9	8	17	27	54	35
West Ham	32	8	10	14	40	58	34
Crystal Palace	34	8	10	16	36	54	34
Swansea	33	8	9	16	27	46	33
Southampton	33	5	13	15	33	53	28
Stoke	33	6	9	18	30	63	27
West Brom	34	4	12	18	27	52	24

---

the Premier League.

Zaha's feet, pace and power are another matter. Albion simply could not handle him in the first half.

Palace, fortunately, also exhibited set-piece charity to help the Seagulls halve the early arrears.

Lewis Dunk, too strong for Mamadou Sakho, met Pascal Gross's corner with a header which Glenn Murray hooked in on the volley from a yard out.

Jose Izquierdo, latching onto Locadia's pass, cut the deficit to one

again in the most prolific first-half fixture in the Premier League this season with a delightful curling finish with his deadly right foot.

As often happens after a rush of goals, that was the end of the scoring, although it should not have been.

Murray, unfortunate with a stretching volley inches wide from a Beram Kayal cross, contrived late-on from two yards out to volley away from and not into the net another volley after Ulloa flicked on another

Kayal cross. Hughton was more concerned about his team giving themselves too much to do.

"They were three poor goals, particularly in this type of game where you know the importance of it," he said,

"It was a problem we had addressed (from corners) so I am annoyed and frustrated. It's difficult to come back from that. At this stage of the season it's the last thing you would want in any game. We know what this game means to our sup-

porters and also what it means as regards points that both clubs need."

Albion will have to pull their socks up to compete with Spurs.

"There won't be one player that doesn't know the situation we're in, doesn't know that we need to get points, and doesn't know what we have to put into the performance against Tottenham," Hughton said.

"Nobody at this club wants to leave it to the last game."

Especially not when it is at Anfield.

Albion ratings ✓

MATHEW RYAN 8/10
Excellent. As at Palace, he ended the first half with a brilliant save low to his left. But that was the only similarity to his shaky opening 45 at Selhurst.

BRUNO 8/10
The returning skipper had his work cut out against Son but blocked some crosses and showed poise and expertise on the ball to get Albion moving.

SHANE DUFFY 8/10
Looked to the heavens in relief when his intended interception sent the ball inches past his own post. Would have been cruel had it gone in as he was excellent.

LEWIS DUNK 8/10
Took an early booking which possibly saved a goal. That didn't stop him sliding into a fierce tackle later in the first half and defending superbly.

GAETAN BONG 7/10
Stretched defensively – and exposed when Spurs broke the deadlock straight after the interval. Warmed Lloris' palms with an on-target first-half drive.

ANTHONY KNOCKAERT 7/10
Looked up for it and saw his deflected effort cause Lloris discomfort. Enjoyed combining with Bruno and Gross and did his defensive chores.

BERAM KAYAL 8/10
Awful early pass could have been so costly but settled in had a terrific game, a real buzzing presence as Spurs looked to play their way through.

DALE STEPHENS 7/10
Worked away in midfield without being able to get on the ball and show his passing range as is often the case.

JOSE IZQUIERDO 7/10
Caught out by Aurier at Wembley in December, this time he turned the tables to force the penalty just when Albion needed it. Otherwise found the right-back hard to beat

PASCAL GROSS 8/10
Flitted in and out but stood up to a huge responsibility from the penalty spot. Involved in some clever creative play when Albion were able to get on the ball.

GLENN MURRAY 7/10
Mainly an evening for getting on the ball and looking to link up with colleagues. Did so to good effect at times in the first half – and again for the score-levelling spot kick.

SUBS
LEO ULLOA: did a decent job protecting possession.
SOLLY MARCH: Brought late energy in attack and defence on the left.

Gross spot on

Seagulls inching to safety after Spurs draw

 Albion..........1
 Tottenham..1

EXACTLY a year on from gaining promotion, Albion earned a precious point towards staying in the Premier League for a second year.

Pascal Gross, taking over penalty duties from Glenn Murray, calmly converted from the spot in the second half, two minutes after Harry Kane gave Tottenham the lead.

Gross is a strong contender to be named player of the season at the awards ceremony tomorrow night.

The German No.10 has been an enormous influence on the quest for safety. He has now scored six goals, all of them at the Amex, to accompany eight assists. Directly and indirectly playing a role in 14 of 32 goals is some contribution for around £3.5 million from unfashionable Ingolstadt.

Albion produced the response Chris Hughton wanted against his old club to a sequence of three defeats and a draw since defeating Arsenal at home last month.

Four points against the North London neighbours has gone a long way towards keeping them up.

It is not Hughton's style to overreact to a setback, so there were only two changes to the team beaten by arch-rivals Crystal Palace at Selhurst Park.

Ezequiel Schelotto, part of the general early defensive malaise in Croydon, made way at right-back for the return of skipper Bruno for the first time since January.

The veteran Spaniard has a good understanding with Anthony Knockaert and it was no surprise to see the Frenchman, brought on in the second half at Palace following suspension, restored to the right flank.

Knockaert made his first home start since last month's win over Arsenal at the expense of record signing Jurgen Locadia.

Mauricio Pochettino rotated his Spurs squad with six changes to the side beaten by champions Manchester City at Wembley at the weekend, a result which ended their 14-match unbeaten run.

Toby Alderweireld, Serge Aurier, Victor Wanyama, Moussa Sissoko, Son Heung-min and Lucas Moura came in for Davinson Sanchez, Kieran Trippier, Eric Dier, Mousa Dembele, Lucas Moura and Dele Alli ahead of Saturday's FA Cup semi-final against Manchester United.

The pattern was soon established, Spurs dominating possession and probing, Albion determined and disciplined. The only real alarm for the Seagulls in the opening quarter of the contest was

Tottenham Hotspur's Harry Kane scores the opening goal at the Amex Pictures: Liz Finlayson/Simon Dack

Mathew Ryan makes a vital save at the end of the first half against Tottenham

Albion's Pascal Gross steps up and buries the equalising penalty against Tottenham

By ANDY NAYLOR
Chief sports reporter

self-inflicted. Beram Kayal's short pass back to Lewis Dunk was intercepted by Moura.

Dunk brought down the Brazilian on the edge of the box, earning a booking from Kevin Friend and presenting Spurs with the sort of opportunity from the resulting free-kick which Christian Eriksen usually exploits.

Not this time. The wall did its job, blocking the normally lethal Dane's drive.

Albion needed to make the most of set-pieces, which they have failed to do often enough this season, and opportunities to hit Tottenham on the counter-attack.

Dunk's header from a Gross corner was grabbed, at the second attempt, by Hugo Lloris. Knockaert took an accidental whack on the nose from Viktor Wanyama's arm when he threatened to break through early on.

He is an effervescent spark at his best and he carried the fight to Tottenham with a solo burst from inside his own half after Jan Vertonghen had a shot blocked.

Knockaert jinked inside the central defender and the shot that followed took a deflection off Ben Davies, forcing Lloris into a diving

as Albion bag point

Pascal Gross celebrates his leveller from the penalty spot with Glenn Murray

Bruno celebrates at the final whistle against Tottenham

referee

Could Kevin Friend have let that late Ryan kick go when Albion seemed to be through? A mixed night but got the yellow card and penalty right. **6**

next up

Burnley v Albion, Premier League, April 28, 3pm

and table

Premier League

	P	W	D	L	F	A	Pts
Man City	33	28	3	2	93	25	87
Man Utd	33	22	5	6	63	26	71
Liverpool	34	20	10	4	78	35	70
Tottenham	34	20	8	6	66	31	68
Chelsea	33	18	6	9	57	33	60
Arsenal	33	16	6	11	62	45	54
Burnley	33	14	10	9	33	29	52
Leicester	33	11	10	12	49	47	43
Everton	34	11	9	14	39	54	42
Newcastle	33	11	8	14	35	42	41
Bournemouth	34	9	11	14	41	56	38
Watford	34	10	7	17	42	60	37
ALBION	**34**	**8**	**12**	**14**	**32**	**47**	**36**
West Ham	33	8	11	14	41	59	35
Huddersfield	34	9	8	17	27	54	35
Crystal Palace	34	8	10	16	36	54	34
Swansea	33	8	9	16	27	46	33
Southampton	33	5	13	15	33	53	28
Stoke	34	6	10	18	31	64	28
West Brom	34	4	12	18	27	52	24

save. At this stage Kane had been patrolled effectively by Dunk and Shane Duffy. Spurs, for all their possession, created little.

Moura produced a routine tip-over for Mathew Ryan, but that was from 25 yards. The main threat closer to goal came from Son down the left. He was a test for Bruno on his comeback.

The captain generally coped well, with the assistance of his team-mates. The South Korean often found himself surrounded by two or three players.

Albion almost shot themselves in the foot again just before half-time. A stray pass back by Knockaert straight to Kane led to another free-kick on the edge of the area.

Kane slipped as Eriksen tapped the ball to him and the shot lacked venom to bother Ryan. Albion's Australian keeper produced a fine stop with his left hand moments later to preserve parity at the interval from Son's effort inside the box after Kane set him up.

The second half started badly, Kane giving Spurs the lead in the 48th minute with a goal largely of Albion's own making.

Gross's pass played Gaetan Bong into trouble and he was dispossessed. A touch of stardust from Son, evading Dunk and Ryan in a tight area, led to Kane driving in his 41st goal in 47 appearances in all competitions, despite Bruno's attempted block off the line.

Albion responded two minutes later. Aurier, who fluked Tottenham's opening goal from a cross when the teams met at Wembley in December, clumsily caught Jose Izquierdo from behind inside the area.

Gross, replacing Murray as penalty taker after the latter's failure in the recent home defeat by Leicester, beat Lloris low to the keeper's right.

It was exactly the boost Albion needed. Falling behind against one of the top six can often be fatal.

Moura fired wide of Ryan's near post when well-placed to restore Tottenham's advantage. An outstretched leg from Duffy also diverted Eriksen's angled drive just wide of the far post as Spurs pressed for a winner. Ryan completed a fine evening's work by holding a shot from Erik Lamela late on.

The**PREM** »

Albion ratings ✓

MATHEW RYAN
Solid again. Repelled two free-kicks from Gudmundsson, the first a helping hand in a scramble, the second a more authentic diving stop. **7**

BRUNO
Captain kept Gudmundsson quiet and the ineffective Lennon after the break. Screwed wide chance on the volley. Went off feeling a hamstring. **7**

SHANE DUFFY
Abrasive ding-dong with former Seagulls Wood and Barnes was right up his street. Plenty of stout heading and blocking inside his own box. **8**

LEWIS DUNK
Vital goal-line block to foil Long, even if he didn't know much about it. Customarily sound in defence and mainly good in possession. **7**

GAETAN BONG
Booed when on the ball throughout by Burnley fans in home town of racism case rival Jay Rodriguez. Responded with typically resolute display. **8**

ANTHONY KNOCKAERT
Buzzed around when he got the chance and did his bit defensively but lacked the conviction of last season when he had a sight of goal. **6**

Leo Ulloa looks downbeat against Burnley in the goalless clash

BERAM KAYAL
Busy game which he relished but would have loved to have made better connection on a chance. Now what happens with Propper available? **7**

DALE STEPHENS
Not inhibited by what looked a harsh booking as he closed on in Barnes. One early pass put his side in trouble but that was the exception. **7**

JOSE IZQUIERDO
One of those games where he always looks like he might make the difference but it never quite happens. **6**

PASCAL GROSS
Prompted, probed and tried the Cruyff turn but nothing ever quite came off. Was it a disguised pass for Ulloa with wide first-half effort? **6**

LEO ULLOA
Delighted to be starting and did what he could to retain possession but it was in a tough assignment and never really had a sight of goal. **6**

SUBS

GLENN MURRAY: Had shot deflected wide. SOLLY MARCH: Tested the defence during a late flurry. EZEQUIEL SCHELOTTO: A capable deputy for the limping Bruno.

Hughton's blast

Seagulls boss labels Bong boos 'shameful'

Burnley	0
Albion	0

WHEN Chris Hughton is outspoken, you know full well something is seriously wrong.

Albion's manager is as respectful as they come, particularly when he talks about the opposition.

For Hughton to brand the behaviour of Burnley fans towards Gaetan Bong as "shameful" is a measure of his disgust.

We should all be disgusted. A reaction against Bong at the spiritual home of Jay Rodriguez was not unexpected.

The West Brom striker is Burnley-born and bred, so Bong was an obvious target after the FA charged Rodriguez with making a racist comment towards him at the Hawthorns in January and an independent commission found the allegation "unproven".

Bong was booed as soon as he touched the ball. That was not entirely surprising, but the boos never stopped. They continued throughout the match, from the first minute to the last.

He was hounded for having the temerity to make a complaint which both the FA and independent commission deemed to be completely in good faith.

The verdict was carefully worded with good reason. Rodriguez was not exonerated and cleared, as he and his camp and supporters would like everyone to believe.

There was not enough transparent evidence for the commission to arrive at a decision either way, because Rodriguez covered his mouth at the crucial moment.

What message does the behaviour of Burnley supporters send out if another player finds himself in the same situation as Bong and also wants to make a complaint in good faith?

Players like 23-year-old Frenchman Georges-Kevin Nkoudou, who joined Burnley on loan from Spurs in January and came on in the second half. They will probably think it is not worth the hassle.

Hughton's post-match comments related to the boos. Two separate allegations have now emerged from Albion supporters that Bong was subjected to monkey chants as he went to take a throw-in during the second half.

If this is true then these individuals have defended 'one of their own', accused of racial abuse, by racially abusing the complainant. You could not make it up.

The FA should investigate these

Shane Duffy gets across to block on the line during the game with Burnley

Burnley players call for a penalty for handball after the goalmouth scramble

Goalkeeper Mathew Ryan spoons the ball off the goaline in an almighty scramble **Pictures: Richard Parkes**

By ANDY NAYLOR
Chief sports reporter

claims and, if proven, demonstrate they are serious about tackling the issue by coming down hard on Burnley.

To his credit, Bong made a big contribution to Albion's first clean sheet since another 0-0 draw at Newcastle at the end of 2017.

He nullified the ineffective Aaron Lennon, who was eventually replaced by Nkoudou, and Joey Gudmundsson after they swapped sides.

It has been a remarkable season for Burnley, now virtually assured of seventh place and Europa League qualification.

To get there, Sean Dyche's side must have demonstrated more quality than they showed against

Albion. Their approach was direct and agricultural. Winning free-kicks in opposition territory is all part of the game plan and difficult to avoid when you are up against the robust pairing of Ashley Barnes and Chris Wood or Sam Vokes.

Shane Duffy and Lewis Dunk dealt well with the former Seagulls. The only time Burnley really threatened was from a Gudmundsson free-kick midway through the first half which provoked an al-

truly speaks volumes

Gaetan Bong heads clear under pressure for Albion against Burnley at Turf Moor

the teams

Albion (4-4-1-1): Ryan; Bruno, Duffy, Dunk, Bong; Knockaert, Stephens, Kayal, Izquierdo; Gross; Ulloa.
Subs: Murray for Ulloa (67), March for Izquierdo (85), Schelotto for Bruno (89), Krul, Goldson, Locadia, Suttner.
Goals: None.
Red cards: None.
Yellow cards: Stephens (41) foul, Murray (70) foul.
Burnley (4-4-2): Pope; Lowton, Tarkowski, Long, Ward; Gudmundsson, Cork, Westwood, Lennon; Barnes, Wood.
Subs: Vokes for Wood (65), Nkoudou for Lennon (71), Hendrick for Westwood (81), Heaton, Taylor, Wells, Bardsley.
Goals: None.
Red cards: None.
Yellow cards: None.
Referee: Roger East (Wiltshire).
Attendance: 19,459 (1,912).

match stats

ALBION		BURNLEY
1	Shots on	4
8	Shots off	6
4	Corners	3
3	Offsides	4
15	Free-kicks conceded	5
56%	Possession	44%

referee

Some question marks over Roger East's decision to penalise and book Dale Stephens as he ran with Ashley Barnes but was right to ignore various appeals when Burnley lofted high balls into the congested penalty area. 7

next up

Albion v Manchester United, Premier League Friday (8pm).

and table

Premier League

	P	W	D	L	F	A	Pts
Man City (C)	35	30	3	2	102	26	93
Man Utd	35	24	5	6	67	27	77
Liverpool	36	20	12	4	80	37	72
Tottenham	34	20	8	6	66	31	68
Chelsea	35	20	6	9	60	34	66
Arsenal	35	17	6	12	67	48	57
Burnley	36	14	12	10	35	32	54
Everton	36	13	9	14	42	54	48
Leicester	35	11	11	13	49	52	44
Newcastle	35	11	8	16	35	44	41
Crystal Palace	36	9	11	16	41	54	38
Bournemouth	36	9	11	16	42	60	38
Watford	35	10	8	17	42	60	38
ALBION	35	8	13	14	32	47	37
West Ham	35	8	11	16	43	67	35
Huddersfield	35	9	8	18	27	56	35
Swansea	35	8	9	18	27	52	33
Southampton	35	6	14	15	35	54	32
Stoke	36	6	12	18	32	65	30
West Brom	36	5	13	18	30	54	28

mighty scramble. Desperate defending by Bong and Mathew Ryan foiled a combination of Barnes and Jack Cork, then Kevin Long's effort from James Tarkowski's back-heel was blocked via the post by Lewis Dunk. The ball appeared to hit Dunk on the arm, but he knew nothing about it and referee Roger East rightly rejected Burnley appeals for a penalty.

Albion were also impotent in attack, despite several promising situations. On-loan Leo Ulloa, preferred to Glenn Murray, looked rusty on his first Premier League start for over a year and they lacked a cutting edge in the final third.

That has been a familiar theme away from the Amex. West Brom's win at Newcastle leaves them as the lowest scorers on their travels, just nine goals in 17 games.

Nevertheless, it was a good and deserved point which has edged the Seagulls even closer to safety.

Although the gap between them and the relegation zone has narrowed to five points as a result of Southampton beating Bournemouth, they benefit from Saints still having to visit fellow strugglers Swansea in the final midweek of the season.

The Welshmen and Huddersfield, who lost at home to Everton, both look vulnerable now.

Much of the focus has been on Albion's daunting finish, Manchester United at home followed by Manchester City and Liverpool away.

Huddersfield, two points worse off with a far inferior goal difference, go to City when they are being presented with the Premier League trophy, then Chelsea still chasing Spurs and Liverpool.

Arsenal at home on the final day appeared to be the saving grace for the West Yorkshiremen. The Gunners have been woeful away, but that fixture has a different complexion now that it will be Arsene Wenger's last in the Premier League.

It will require an improbable set of results for Albion to not be safe by then.

Albion ratings ✓

MATHEW RYAN 9/10

Had to wait for serious action but plunged to his right and had strong arms to repel Rashford's shot. Always calm and cool both on the deck and in the air.

BRUNO 9/10

Was keen to gallop forward in support of Knockaert. But this was a night of trademark defence and composure. Nicking the ball off Matic was a high spot.

SHANE DUFFY 9/10

Not for the first time, defended to great effect but should have scored with a header from a set-piece.

LEWIS DUNK 9/10

Got a very hard head in the way of a very hard volley from Rashford, to sum up a night of hard-nosed defending.

GAETAN BONG 9/10

Such a competitor. Defended strongly throughout and shrugged off a knock sustained at the end of the first half.

ANTHONY KNOCKAERT 9/10

Really looked up for it. Head down at times but such a livewire, both on his wing and drifting a long way infield.

DALE STEPHENS 9/10

Razor sharp into the tackle as Albion tried to ensure United's midfielders had an uncomfortable night.

DAVY PROPPER 9/10

Steely graft on a testing night and a touch of silk with the carefully weighted and timed pass for Izquierdo ahead of the opening goal.

JOSE IZQUIERDO 9/10

Loved getting the ball to his feet and running at defenders. Saw goalkeeper De Gea get fingertips to a first-half dipper.

PASCAL GROSS 9/10

What a way to cap his dream debut season at the Amex. A header which got there by an inch or two to cap his inventive night.

GLENN MURRAY 9/10

It took a super save to keep out his fabulous long-range effort which would have caught many keepers unawares. Battled away.

SUBS
BERAM KAYAL: Sent on for midfield strength.
SOLLY MARCH: Did his bit defending.
LEO ULLOA: On right at the end.

Albion over the

Ecstasy at Amex as Seagulls are safe

 Albion..........1
Man Utd......0

WHAT a way to do it.

Albion ensured they will be playing Manchester United again in the Premier League next season with a stirring victory over Jose Mourinho's side.

Pascal Gross was the hero again with their second-half winner.

It was well-deserved too. Chris Hughton's Seagulls were the better side, especially in the first half when David De Gea kept them at bay with a series of saves.

Albion now head to champions Manchester City and Champions League finalists Liverpool safe from the bottom three, as Swansea and Southampton still have to play each other.

Hughton, taking charge of his 150th league game with Albion, restored Davy Propper in midfield after his three-match ban and brought back Glenn Murray for Leo Ulloa following the 0-0 draw at Burnley.

Mourinho made half-a-dozen amendments to the United team that snatched a late victory over Arsenal at Old Trafford.

Romelu Lukaku's absence with an ankle injury sustained against the Gunners was well-documented during the build-up.

Alexis Sanchez was missing from the line-up as well through injury.

That left a front three of Juan Mata, Marcus Rashford and Anthony Martial, with only former Seagull Jesse Lingard for back-up on the bench.

In the centre of United's defence, Marcos Rojo was drafted in for his first appearance since February.

Albion survived an early alarm after Shane Duffy blocked off Rashford 20 yards out.

Rashford's resulting free-kick was touched in by Marouane Fellaini, United's matchwinner against Arsenal, but he was narrowly offside.

The Seagulls were not perturbed. Anthony Knockaert buzzed with intent, Dale Stephens relished his midfield exchanges with Paul Pogba.

Stephens shot wide to climax an attacking flurry, Jose Izquierdo had an effort blocked after a dazzling run by Knockaert and a low drive by Pascal Gross forced David De Gea, United's Player of the Year, into a routine gather.

Albion continued to carry the game to United, who were too pedestrian when they attacked.

Murray, needing one goal to emulate the watching Peter Ward's tally of 95 for the club, was denied by a fine save by De Gea.

Murray struck instantly from 25 yards after Propper won possession. De Gea was at full-stretch to keep it out with his right hand.

The threat from United at that stage had been minimal. Lewis Dunk, typically determined in his defending, headed clear a vicious Rashford volley.

Dunk had a let-off soon after when a combination of imprecise control and a slip from Gaetan Bong's throw let in Rashford. He delayed and the opportunity went begging.

De Gea was much busier than Mathew Ryan. The Spaniard fingertipped over Izquierdo's shot from outside the box and from Gross's ensuing corner, Duffy steered wide a header which just eluded Murray at the far post.

Albion, knowing the prize at stake for only a second victory in 19 meetings with United, looked a lot hungrier than their illustrious visitors.

De Gea was called into action once more to block Gross by his near post after Knockaert threaded the German through.

Pogba typified United's ineptitude just before half-time with a gallop ruined by a horribly overhit pass, which produced a glare

By ANDY NAYLOR
Chief sports reporter

Pascal Gross scores against Manchester United but only after goalline technology was required

Pascal Gross is denied by Manchester United goalkeeper David De Gea in the first half

Pascal Gross races away after scoring for Albion against Manchester United Pictures: Simon Dack/Liz Finlayson

line in survival race

Albion's Pascal Gross, right, celebrates with Anthony Knockaert afte scoring the winner in a famous win over Manchester United that ensured safety

the teams

Albion (4-4-1-1): Ryan; Bruno, Duffy, Dunk, Bong; Knockaert, Stephens, Propper, Izquierdo (March 88); Gross (Kayal 84); Murray (Ulloa 90+2).

Subs not used: Krul, Goldson, Schelotto, Locadia.

Goal: Gross 57.

Yellow cards: Gross (67) foul, Murray foul.

Manchester Utd (4-3-3): De Gea; Darmian (Shaw 68), Smalling, Rojo (McTominay 76); Young; Matic, Fellaini (Lingard 68), Pogba; Mata, Rashford, Martial.

Subs not used: Romero, Bailly, Lindelof, Herrera.

Goals: None

Yellow card: None

Referee: Craig Pawson (South Yorkshire)

Attendance: 30,611.

stats

ALBION		MAN UTD
4	Shots on	3
7	Shots off	13
5	Corners	6
1	Offsides	2
5	Free-kicks conceded	3
32%	Possession	68%

Goalline technology ensured a famous win for the Seagulls

ref watch

Craig Pawson might have given a penalty when Anthony Knockaert went down but had as decent night. **7**

Bruno celebrates at the end

next up

Manchester City v Albion, Premier League, Wednesday (8pm).

and table

Premier League

	P	W	D	L	F	A	Pts
Man City	35	30	3	2	102	26	93
Man Utd	36	24	5	7	67	28	77
Liverpool	36	20	12	4	80	37	72
Tottenham	35	21	8	6	68	31	71
Chelsea	35	20	6	9	60	34	66
Arsenal	35	17	6	12	67	48	57
Burnley	36	14	12	10	35	32	54
Everton	36	13	9	14	42	54	48
Leicester	35	11	11	13	49	52	44
Newcastle	35	11	8	16	35	44	41
ALBION	**36**	**9**	**13**	**14**	**33**	**47**	**40**
Crystal Palace	36	9	11	16	41	54	38
Bournemouth	36	9	11	16	42	60	38
Watford	36	10	8	18	42	62	38
West Ham	35	8	11	16	43	67	35
Huddersfield	35	9	8	18	27	56	35
Swansea	35	8	9	18	27	52	33
Southampton	35	6	14	15	35	54	32
Stoke	36	6	12	18	32	65	30
West Brom	35	5	13	18	30	54	28

of despair from Mourinho.

The only disappointment for Hughton was that Albion, well-drilled and cohesive by contrast, were not ahead.

United re-emerged with more purpose and tempo to their passing, but Albion stunned them with a well-merited breakthrough in the 57th minute.

Izquierdo's cross-shot was parried by De Gea and Gross's header was hooked clear on the line by the airborne Rojo.

There was a delay before referee Craig Pawson awarded the goal, verified by goalline technology.

Gross's seventh of an influential debut campaign, all of them at home, had the Amex bouncing.

They scented a famous victory, but there was still work to do.

Ryan parried a crisply struck 20-yarder from Rashford as Mourinho rang the changes, introducing first Lingard and Luke Shaw, then Scott McTominay.

Nemanja Matic, scorer of the clinching goal in Albion's 2-0 exit from the FA Cup at Old Trafford in the quarter-finals in March, dropped back to centre-half alongside Chris Smalling.

Albion counterpart Dunk was the victim of an unfortunate own goal, a deflection he could do nothing about, which gave United victory in the League meeting in November.

The Seagulls were in sight of sweet revenge, thanks to Gross's knack of being in the right place in the final third to make an impact. He has also contributed eight assists.

Gross departed to a standing ovation, replaced by Beram Kayal.

Hearts were in mouths when Lingard, linking up with Rashford, fired wide inside the area when well-placed to equalise as the minutes ticked by.

The Seagulls' rearguard action in the closing moments ended, fittingly, with Players' Player of The Season Dunk powering clear a header from inside his own box.

Albion ratings ✓

MATHEW RYAN 7/10

In the right place to block from Fernandinho in the second half although arguably did even better to prod the subsequent back pass clear.

BRUNO 7/10

A mixed time facing the toughest assignment of the night against Sane out wide. Looked good on the ball.

SHANE DUFFY 8/10

Saved a goal early on by blocking from Gundogan and got in plenty of timely interventions and interceptions.

LEWIS DUNK 7/10

Emerged with credit. Some good defending when City found way through with their patient passing.

GAETAN BONG 5/10

Given a really tough time by City's attackers down his flank, notably on both their first-half goals.

ANTHONY KNOCKAERT 6/10

Looked right up for it again and played a clever part in the first-half equaliser. But should have scored later and was slow to react on City's third goal.

DALE STEPHENS 6/10

Chasing and harrying for most of the night as City monopolised possession. Found Sane an elusive opponent when he drifted infield.

DAVY PROPPER 6/10

Great footwork and composure for the first-half leveller after his weak tackle had been a reason why Sane set up the night's first goal for Danilo.

JOSE IZQUIERDO 5/10

Had a shot spilled by Bravo. Otherwise precious little seen of him, either attacking or helping out Bong going the other way.

PASCAL GROSS 6/10

Not much chance to create. Might have done more to stop Sane right at the start of the move for the night's first goal.

LEO ULLOA 6/10

Failure to hold the ball up was at the origin of City's first goal. But he did superbly at both the start and end of the move for the Seagulls' reply.

SUBS

BERAM KAYAL: Part of a double switch straight after City's third goal.
JURGEN LOCADIA: Little chance to shine after replacing Ulloa.
SOLLY MARCH: Sent out on the left late on.

Records fall as

Defeat but no disgrace against the champions

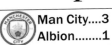

Man City....3
Albion........1

ALBION were well beaten by Pep Guardiola's runaway champions in their penultimate game of the season – but they escaped with honour preserved.

With only Sunday's visit to Liverpool remaining, Chris Hughton's Seagulls have still not lost by more than two goals in an away game throughout their debut campaign in the Premier League.

They were always second-best against a City line-up showing eight changes but had the comfort of on-loan Leo Ulloa's first top flight goal for 17 months which briefly gave them hope in the first half.

There was a singular change to the side that secured survival with victory against the red half of Manchester at the Amex, Ulloa taking over from Glenn Murray up front.

Yaya Toure captained City on his farewell appearance, Vincent Kompany stepping aside in honour of the legendary midfielder despite his return to the defence from injury.

The list of absentees for the champions was impressive, no Kyle Walker, John Stones, Nicolas Otamendi, David Silva, Raheem Sterling or Sergio Aguero. Kevin De Bruyne was among the substitutes.

Albion formed a guard of honour for Toure and his team-mates before kick-off.

City wasted no time in exerting pressure with their silky brand of pass and move, combined with a voracious work ethic to regain possession as quickly as possible and as high up the pitch as possible.

Albion, soon dropping deep inside their own territory, needed Shane Duffy to rescue them from an early deficit. The Irishman blocked Ilkay Gundogan's shot from eight yards from Fernandinho's low cross.

The reprieve was shortlived, the Seagulls falling behind in the 16th minute to a goal expertly fashioned by Leroy Sane. The young German winger, inside his own half, exchanged passes with Fernandinho before a spearing surge through the middle cut Albion open.

The pass was perfectly weighted inside Gaetan Bong for Danilo to run onto and slide past Mathew Ryan. It was a record-equalling thrust, City's 103rd goal of the season emulating Chelsea's tally in 2009-10.

That could have been the signal for the floodgates to open, but Albion had other ideas. They were

Albion striker Leo Ulloa rises to nod a header home against champions Manchester City at the Etihad

Anthony Knockaert shows his anguish after missing a great chance to level at 2-1 Pictures: Richard Parkes

Goalkeeper Mathew Ryan is beaten by Danilo's effort as Manchester City open their account

By ANDY NAYLOR
Chief sports reporter

level four minutes later, courtesy of a move started by Anthony Knockaert with a pass which released Davy Propper.

Keeper Bravo, like Toure making his first Premier League start of the season, came off his line and forced the Dutchman away

from goal to the lefthand edge of the area.

Propper kept his composure and, with Bravo stranded, crossed for Ulloa to nod in his first Premier League goal since scoring for Leicester at Stoke in December 2016.

The unexpected equaliser was a welcome boost for Albion, but it did little to knock City out of their measured stride.

Jesus hit the side-netting from Toure's cross to the near post before Bernardo Silva restored their

lead in the 34th minute.

Sane was the provider again, this time with a cross which reached Silva beyond the far post. Instant control and a shot through the legs of Bong past Ryan eclipsed Chelsea's haul of goals.

It was Sane's 14th assist, one adrift of team-mate De Bruyne at the top of that particular Premier League table.

Albion reached the interval without suffering further damage.

They were still in the game at that stage and Ulloa's goal finally

City sink Seagulls

Albion's Leo Ulloa celebrates scoring the leveller at the Etihad Stadium

took their away total for the season into double figures.

There was no respite in the pattern once the second half was underway. Albion continued to dig in as City pressed and probed for a two-goal cushion.

It was difficult for Albion to escape from their own territory, with Pascal Gross forced deep to help out and Ulloa isolated.

City's anthem, 'Blue Moon', rang out around the Etihad as they nearly ex-tended their lead.

Fernandinho's snapshot inside the box was blocked uncomfortably by Ryan. The Australian's follow-up clear-ance only went as far as Sane, but Albion survived.

They could have been back on terms before the hour. Jose Izquierdo's an-gled drive was spilled by Bravo and Danilo then made a mess of clearing his lines.

The ball fell invitingly for Knockaert, but the French-man fired over from close range. Spurred on by Knock-aert, Albion enjoyed a mini-spell after that. Danilo had to be vigilant to leap and intercept a Dale Stephens pass which would have sent Izquierdo clear.

They remained in conten-tion until the 73rd minute, when they fell asleep at a corner and were punished ruthlessly. Gundogan fed it short to Sane and he picked out Fernandinho to sweep City further ahead with a first-time shot.

That completed a hat-trick of assists for Sane and took the contest out of Al-bion's reach. It was only the second time they have con-ceded three goals away from the Amex after the early ca-pitulation at Crystal Palace.

Hughton rang the chang-es, introducing Beram Kay-al, Jurgen Locadia and Solly March for Gross, Ulloa and Izquierdo. City fans were desperate for a Toure goal to round off his career with the club, but he could only

shoot straight into the arms of Ryan after an exchange of passes with Sane. Toure departed to hugs from his team-mates and a rapturous reception.

Two more records set by Chelsea were broken by City with their 31st win and 97 points. A Danilo free-kick, curled against the crossbar, spared Albion their heaviest away defeat of the season. The only number that mat-ters to them is that they can-not finish lower than 15th.

Albion ratings ✓

MATHEW RYAN
Conceded four, of which none were his fault, and made several saves, at least three of which looked improbable to say the least. **9**

EZEQUIEL SCHELOTTO
A chaotic afternoon. Given a torrid time from the first minute by Mane and his blunder teed up Firmino for a clear chance in second period. **4**

SHANE DUFFY
Lucky not to concede a penalty at 0-0 but also got in some great defending from the early stages, notably a goal-line clearance from Salah. **6**

LEWIS DUNK
Albion's usually strong back line really struggled with Liverpool's pace, movement and intensity – and that included the skipper. **5**

GAETAN BONG
Has ended his good season with a tough week. Given the expected hard time by Salah but hung in there grimly (quite literally at times). **5**

BERAM KAYAL
Another tough assignment for the Israeli to add to Spurs (twice), Chelsea, Everton, Palace and Burnley away. **5**

Solly March spent much of the game defending

DALE STEPHENS
Will not thank Adam Lallana for catching him as soon as he came off the bench for his 100th Liverpool league appearance. **6**

DAVY PROPPER
Tough for the Dutchman to get a foothold in the middle of the park, with Liverpool so unrelenting. Tried to stem the flow. **6**

ANTHONY KNOCKAERT
Has been reinvigorated since his red card at Everton. The Frenchman had little opportunity to test Robertson defensively on this occasion. **6**

JURGEN LOCADIA
Welcome to Anfield. Record signing cut an isolated figure as a centre-forward, up against van Dijk and Lovren. Withdrawn. **5**

SOLLY MARCH
Did far more defending than attacking against Alexander-Arnold. One-finger salute to pals in crowd, caught by TV, merely a misunderstanding. **6**

SUBS
PASCAL GROSS: Cause was already lost.
GLENN MURRAY: Ditto Gross.
CONNOR GOLDSON: Rare minutes for the injured Duffy.

Rampant Reds

Tough end to season takes a toll at Anfield

Liverpool.....4
Albion..........0

THANK goodness the job was done and Albion were not still in jeopardy in the final two fixtures of the season.

Beating a stodgy Manchester United to secure safety at the Amex, where they are capable of giving anyone a game, is one thing.

Facing free-flowing Manchester City and Liverpool away twice in swift succession is quite another.

The challenge, not surprisingly, was well beyond Chris Hughton's team, an aggregate of seven goals conceded and one scored in the toughest of finishes to what, nevertheless, has been a memorable debut campaign amongst the elite.

Albion have ended it seven points and three places clear of an immediate return to the grind of the Championship. Everyone would have settled for that in August.

Liverpool, meanwhile, head into the Champions League final against Real Madrid later this month with qualification for next season's competition already assured.

As it transpired it would have made no difference if the Seagulls had inflicted their first defeat at Anfield this season, courtesy of Chelsea's demise at Newcastle, although Liverpool were never in the remotest danger of such a surprising denouement.

Hughton's last day line-up was designed to freshen the team up with an injection of pace after their exertions at Manchester City.

Ezequiel Schelotto, Beram Kayal, Solly March and Jurgen Locadia came in for Bruno, Pascal Gross, the injured Jose Izquierdo and Leo Ulloa.

Nineteen of Albion's 34 Premier League goals were on the bench, where Gross and Glenn Murray were accompanied by Leo Ulloa.

The Argentinian missed out on his 50th league start for the club, spread over two spells, following his equaliser in the 3-1 defeat at City.

Jurgen Klopp made only two changes to the Liverpool side beaten at Chelsea, one of them enforced by an injury to James Milner which is not expected to keep the tireless midfielder out of the Champions League final against Real Madrid on May 26.

Any suggestion Liverpool would be distracted by their big date in Kiev, rather than concentrating on the point they theoretically needed prior to kick-off to secure Champions League qualification, were soon dismissed.

They swarmed all over Albion from the outset with high-pressing intensity and speed of movement in the final third. The Seagulls simply could not cope.

There is no shame in that. Much

By ANDY NAYLOR
Chief sports reporter

better sides throughout Europe have suffered in similar fashion, although Albion needed to be better in possession to give themselves breathing room.

There are many easier places for ex-Evertonian Shane Duffy to have made the 200th start of his career.

In the first quarter of the contest alone the Irishman, so formidable with Lewis Dunk at the heart of the defence, made an important block, got away with an unintentional handball inside the box, almost gifted a goal to Dominic Solanke and escaped again when bringing down Mo Salah inside

the area.

Albion needed a Friend. They had one in the shape of referee Kevin, who denied Liverpool a penalty.

It was only a matter of time before wave after wave of red attacks were rewarded and by who else.

Trent Alexander-Arnold strode forward, fed Solanke who in turn found Salah.

The Egyptian buried himself into Liverpool history with another clinical finish, his 32nd Premier League goal of the campaign taking him past the club record of Luis Suarez in 2013-14.

Beram Kayal tackles Trent Alexander-Arnold
Pictures: Richard Parkes

Centre-half Shane Duffy clears off the line as Liverpool try to force in the ball after a Mathew Ryan save

Lewis Dunk makes a desperate attempt to clear Andy Robertson's shot on the line but can't stop the fourth

roll over the Seagulls

Premier League Golden Boot winner Mo Salah takes on the Albion defence

the teams

Albion (4-3-3): Ryan; Schelotto, Duffy, Dunk, Bong; Kayal, Stephens, Propper; Knockaert, Locadia, March.
Subs: Gross for Kayal (57), Murray for Locadia (57), Goldson for Duffy (71), Krul, Bruno, Goldson, Suttner, Ulloa.
Goals: None.
Red cards: None.
Yellow cards: None.
Liverpool (4-2-1-3): Karius; Alexander-Arnold, Lovren, van Dijk, Robertson; Henderson, Wijnaldum; Firmino; Salah, Solanke, Mane.
Subs: Lallana for Mane (73), Ings for Firmino (83), Woodburn for Salah (83), Mignolet, Clyne, Klavan, Moreno.
Goals: Salah (26) Lovren (40), Solanke (53), Robertson (86).
Red cards: None.
Yellow cards: None.
Referee: Kevin Friend (Leicester).
Attendance: 50,752.

match stats

ALBION		LIVERPOOL
1	Shots on	11
1	shots off	11
3	Corners	7
1	Offside	1
6	Free-kicks conceded	3
28%	Possession	72%

referee

Kevin Friend made a few enemies on the Kop and there were two or three decisions which seemed to go against the hosts in the first half, notably his refusal to award a penalty for Duffy's slide into Salah at 0-0. **5**

next match

Premier League, August 11.

final table

Premier League

	P	W	D	L	F	A	Pts
Man City (C)	38	32	4	2	106	27	100
Man Utd	38	25	6	7	68	28	81
Tottenham	38	23	8	7	74	36	77
Liverpool	38	21	12	5	84	38	75
Chelsea	38	21	7	10	62	38	70
Arsenal	38	19	6	13	74	51	63
Burnley	38	14	12	12	36	39	54
Everton	38	13	10	15	44	58	49
Leicester	38	12	11	15	56	60	47
Newcastle	38	12	8	18	39	47	44
Crystal Palace	38	11	11	16	45	55	44
Bournemouth	38	11	11	16	45	61	44
West Ham	38	10	12	16	48	68	42
Watford	38	11	8	19	44	64	41
ALBION	**38**	**9**	**13**	**16**	**34**	**54**	**40**
Huddersfield	38	9	10	19	28	58	37
Southampton	38	7	15	16	37	56	36
Swansea (R)	38	8	9	21	28	56	33
Stoke (R)	38	7	12	19	35	68	33
West Brom (R)	38	6	13	19	31	56	31

It should have been 2-0 moments later. Sadio Mane was clean through as Albion looked in vain for an offside flag. He should have scored himself but tried to square for a Salah tap-in.

Mathew Ryan's smothering save and Duffy's goal-line clearance from Salah's follow-up merely delayed the inevitable.

The routine nature of Liverpool's second goal, five minutes from the interval, was agitating, Dejan Lovren soaring unchallenged to head in Andy Robertson's left-wing cross from seven yards.

The feted Liverpool front trio of Salah, Mane and Firmino was disrupted by the inclusion of Solanke, with Firmino reverting to a more withdrawn role.

It made no discernible difference to their potency.

Solanke struck the third eight minutes into the restart, firing into the roof of the net via another incisive burst by Salah.

Roberston completed the scoring four minutes from time, lashing in when Dunk cleared a cross to him.

Dunk actually got the last touch, a desperate attempt to head the ball off the line. He certainly would not wish to claim a hat-trick of own goals against Liverpool, having put through his own net in each of the two previous meetings.

They ended in a 6-1 defeat in the FA Cup at Anfield under Gus Poyet and a 5-1 drubbing at the Amex in December.

Liverpool were flattered on that occasion. Not this time. Only a combination of several fine saves by Ryan and wasteful finishing rescued Albion from further damage.

It was still their heaviest away defeat of the season. They had not previously been beaten by more than a two-goal margin.

Then again, thankfully, they do not have to face Liverpool every week. Duffy departed, eventually, before the end following a heavy fall on his back as he headed clear.

It was a sobering afternoon in the Merseyside sunshine as well for record signing Locadia, used as a centre-forward by Hughton for the first time in the Premier League but withdrawn before the hour.

He saw nothing like this with PSV Eindhoven in Eredivisie.

There should be better to come from him next season, when Albion will be visiting Anfield again.

That is all that matters, not a chastening finale.

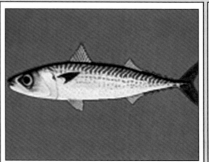

LOTTO
Lotto Saturday, April 28: 03, 11, 37, 38, 43, 44 Bonus: 20

Thunderball, 02, 13, 21, 25, 30 Thunderball: 14

Lotto Wednesday, May 2: 04, 08, 10, 26, 38, 48 Bonus: 41

Thunderball, 01, 09, 20, 22, 24 Thunderball: 01

EUROMILLIONS
Friday, April 27: 12, 24, 40, 41, 46 Lucky Stars: 05, 12

Tuesday, May 1: 06, 15, 17, 42, 48 Lucky Stars: 04, 06

TO CONTACT US:
NEWSDESK: 01273 021370
SWITCHBOARD: 01273 021400
HOME DELIVERY: 0800 731 4900
or deliveries@nqe.com

THE ARGUS
Dolphin House,
2-5 Manchester Street,
Brighton BN2 1TF

EDITOR Arron Hendy
01273 021372
arron.hendy@theargus.co.uk

HEAD OF ADVERTISING Richard Harmer
01273 021426
richard.harmer@theargus.co.uk

Amazing

By Amir Razavi
At the Amex
amir.razavi@theargus.co.uk

IT WAS hardly the Great Escape, though the song from that famous film rang out after Albion sealed their safety in English football's top flight with a 1-0 win against the mighty Manchester United at the American Express Community Stadium .

Chants of 'we are staying up' were being sung out by the Albion faithful as the match neared it's end, bringing to an end any lingering fears of relegation to the Championship.

In truth they were already looking safe but while it was still mathematically possible that they could go down the nerves were still there among the supporters.

Thankfully for them it was a different matter on the pitch last night as the team were as cool as a cucumber and good value against a Manchester United team that lacked spirit and energy.

Shane Goble, watching from the heights of the West Stand, was ecstatic as the full-time whistle went.

He said: "It's not far behind the feeling against Wigan last year, when we were promoted. It's great revenge for 1983, too, when they beat us in the FA Cup final. We were favourites to go down, but we have proven everyone wrong. I thought we were safe, but obviously it wasn't certain. To do it against the second-best team in the country as well, it's amazing."

Argus editor Arron Hendy said: "The wonderful supporters deserved a special night and that was what they got. A year ago we enjoyed some momentous scenes after getting promotion and staying in the division must be seen as just as special. It has been a momentous and historic season and Chris Hughton, Paul Barber, Tony Bloom and everyone else associated with the club must be very proud."

Joyous scenes at The Amex

The Argus

TODAY

Summary: A dry day with pleasant sunshine and variable cloud, and light winds. Feeling warm in the sunshine, but cooler near coasts. Maximum Temperature 19°C.

Time		🌡	☂	💨
00:00	🌙	11	<5%	5
03:00	🌙	9	<5%	7
06:00	☀	10	<5%	8
09:00	☀	15	<5%	8
12:00	☀	18	<5%	9
15:00	☀	19	<5%	8
18:00	☀	17	<5%	9
21:00	🌙	12	<5%	9
00:00	🌙	10	<5%	9

Crawley
Haywards Heath
Burgess Hill
Lewes
Chichester Hove Brighton
Worthing
Eastbourne

Weather Watch

5 DAY FORECAST

		MAX	MIN
Saturday	☀	19	9
Sunday	☀	19	10
Monday	☀	19	11
Tuesday	☀	18	10
Wednesday	⛅	14	9

UK & EUROPE

	MAX	MIN
AMSTERDAM	19	8
ATHENS	28	17
BARCELONA	21	14
CYPRUS	32	17
DUBLIN	19	9
FARO	21	15
LONDON	21	9
PARIS	23	12
ROME	22	13
TENERIFE	19	16

DAYLIGHT TIMES
Sunrise 5.28am   Sunset 8.27pm

Tides (high in metres)

BRIGHTON – 01.55 (5.8); 14.21 (5.7)
Tomorrow – 02.28 (5.5); 15.03 (5.4)
CHICHESTER – 02.21 (4.4); 14.51 (4.3)
Tomorrow – 02.57 (4.2); 15.32 (4.1)
LITTLEHAMPTON – 02.00 (5.2); 14.26 (5.1)
Tomorrow – 02.33 (4.9); 15.05 (4.8)
NEWHAVEN – 01.49 (6.1); 14.13 (5.9)
Tomorrow – 02.25 (5.7); 14.53 (5.6)
SHOREHAM – 01.55 (5.7); 14.20 (5.5)
Tomorrow – 02.27 (5.3); 14.58 (5.2)

Reproduced from Admiralty EasyTide Prediction Programme by permission of the Controller of Her Majesty's Stationery Office and the UK Hydrographic Office (www.ukho.gov.uk)

WIND – Light to gentle breeze
Sea – Smooth or slight
VISIBILITY – Good

Albion seal safety

The fans go wild

Brighton celebrate after Pascal Gross heads Pictures: Simon Dack

SPOTLIGHT**ARGUS**

Albion secure top

By Amir Razavi
Reporter
amir.razavi@theargus.co.uk

ALBION fans reeled in the glory of Premier League safety last night at the Amex as they beat Manchester United in a historic victory.

The Seagulls marked their last home game of the season with a 1-0 win against the most decorated team in the English game, securing top-flight football for another year.

Some supporters flooded the pitch to celebrate with their heroes after the landmark result.

As kick-off dawned closer, the swarms of Albion fans in their blue and white colours, from Brighton town centre to the Amex, grew greater.

The weather was fitting in the build-up, too, with the sun glistening over the stadium ahead of bank holiday weekend.

Beneath the chants of "we are staying up", there was tension as the clock ticked down, the 30,611-strong crowd in sweats as Premier League status edged closer.

That was until the final whistle, and the crowd erupted as they referee blew full-time.

The moment did not get to fans' heads as they geared up for a match which held such huge significance to everyone involved with Albion.

Liz Costa, vice-chairwoman of Albion's Supporters' Club, has been

> ❝
> **I would still be doing it if we were in the Championship**
> ❞

unfazed by the opposition her side have come up against this year.

She believes her beloved Seagulls are among the top 20 clubs in the country purely on merit.

She said: "This season is a tribute to Mr Chris Hughton and the way he has kept the team going.

"We've done an awful lot better people gave us credit for and, actually, better than I thought we would do.

"We've done it with limited resources compared to the rest of the league, too.

"In some games, we've come up against teams who have one player who costs more than our entire squad.

"We are here on merit.

"I think we have been very good against a number of the big teams.

"We could do the same against Manchester United.

"For the fans at the final home game of the season, they are all there because they want to be."

Liz, though, has not been overly-impressed with the Premier League as a whole.

"It is not the most amazing league to be a part of," she said.

"They are all overpaid football-

Brighton fans before the Premier League match between Brighton and Hove Albion and Manchester United at the American Express Community

ers.

"We are doing it our own way."

In true Albion style, they made fans bite their nails right down to the wire – but it was certainly worth it – and what a way to mark the night after the 21st anniversary of that magical night away at Hereford, when they nicked a draw to stay in the Football League.

You would think fans would have been tense beforehand. But not Liz, or the rest of the faithful we spoke to, however.

They were simply cherishing the moment they all, along with the club, deserve.

She said: "They are just another football team as far as I am concerned.

"There are 11 players on each side who play football.

"You cannot be afraid of them.

"We have gone into every game with no fear, and I think we have kept to that concept.

"We are all just playing the same game."

Whether Albion won, lost or drew, the feeling of the evening — and the season as a whole – will be something that will stick with the thousands of Seagulls fans.

That is from the ones chugging back beer watching from a pub to the season ticket holders who help pack the Amex every home game.

Someone who gets to games with a different kind of ticket is Thomas Smith.

The 19-year-old, a lifelong fan from Haywards Heath, moved to

Newquay in Cornwall last year.

He hops on a plane to watch Albion play their home matches – and has not missed one game since his move.

Thomas, whose first Seagulls game was a 2009 League One clash against Oldham at Withdean, said: "I do it because it's my main passion and it's worth spending the money on.

"I love coming here to watch them.

"I would still be doing it if we

flight status

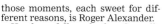

Brighton fans before the Premier League match between Brighton and Hove Albion and Manchester United at the American Express Community

Another historic day as Albion Prem safe

By Amir Razavi
Reporter

LAST night's game against Manchester United signified just how far Albion have come in the past 21 years.

Thursday marked the 21st anniversary of the crucial away draw against Hereford at their 8,000-odd capacity Edgar Street ground.

That draw clinched Football League safety for the Seagulls and, as many say, probably saved the club from sinking into the abyss.

It was a completely different narrative under the floodlights of the 30,750-seater Amex stadium last night.

Albion were playing against one of the greatest teams in modern football history for the third time this season – playing host to some of the most expensive players of all time.

A rather different setting to the last-gasp 1-1 draw in the old Division Two on May 3, 1997.

One fan who has tasted both of those moments, each sweet for different reasons, is Roger Alexander.

He has followed the Seagulls for the past 55 years, so has been through the ups and downs – and the rest.

Roger, 69, said: "The season has been great to watch – some of the football played in the Premier League is sensational.

"Manchester United, with their background and experience, are one of the best teams to watch.

"I was at the Hereford game with my two boys, and at the Doncaster game the week before at the Goldstone. It was magical."

Roger travelled from 117-mile trip from Rugby in Warwickshire to watch his side – a recurring theme among the Seagulls' faithful, with many spectators travelling from far and wide to support their team.

The memories that came with that special point at Hereford, one week after the Seagulls took to the Goldstone turf for the last time, continue to linger in the front of Albion fans' heads.

Each fan, no doubt, has their own unique memory of the day when they watched Robbie Reinelt bag the equaliser to send the hosts down a division, such as Roger spending it with his sons.

Supporter Joanne Thick felt compelled to do something to mark the magical season in some way.

So she named her child after one of Albion's favourite sons.

The 50-year-old, from Hove, said: "I named my son after Dick Knight, who was obviously the chairman at the time. He was born in 1997, the year we stayed up. I said I would do something to mark it."

were in the Championship."

Thomas will be on his way to Merseyside to watch Albion take on Liverpool, their second-to-last match in the Premier League.

He was at last night's game with his mother, Andrea, who has promised him a season ticket for next year.

It was a true thriller for the fans as their team overcame a side they failed to beat on two occasions this season.

Third time lucky.

Business as usual in match build-up

ALBION consulted with Chris Hughton as they prepared for the big night off the pitch.

The result was one which, in hindsight, you will have probably noticed as you went into the Amex but might not have struck you at the time.

It was the final home game of a momentous season.

But there were no flags, no ceremony, no speeches, no opera singers, nothing whatsoever out of the ordinary.

It could have been Watford in December or Swansea in February for all the pomp and extra touches laid on.

The whole matchday was designed to be just like every other home fixture this season.

Players were to notice nothing different.

Chief executive Paul Barber said: "We agreed we would stick exactly to the usual matchday routine.

"Had we already assured safety before the match, maybe we would have done something different.

"We spoke to Chris about it. We have a good home record and routine which he likes.

"We briefed the staff to do nothing different for this game. Nothing different in the way they treated the players.

"The media work was to be nothing different.

"Chris was keen for the players not to feel the slightest difference to a normal home game."

Albion went through their shape and final preparations at the training complex on Thursday and had no distractions of players battling against injury or missing through suspension.

They had known a win would assure safety from the time Chelsea won at Swansea while they were travelling home from the 0-0 draw at Burnley.

Barber saw them last on Wednesday. He said: "What came across was a sense of calm and confidence – no hype.

"They knew we would do it if we won, they knew it was a big game.

"They were just focused and very determined to get the result."

THE **PLAN**

By BRIAN OWEN
Albion reporter
brian.owen@theargus.co.uk

ALBION are safe – thanks to a win over Manchester United and a gameplan they tried and trusted.

The Seagulls hassled and harried United out of their stride, restricted them to very few chances and played some good football themselves.

And, for the fourth time in their seven home wins, they went ahead for good in the period after half-time.

There was a feeling of belief that this could be a special night from the moment Cesc Fabregas's goal for Chelsea at Swansea the previous Saturday meant a win would secure elite status.

It was set up perfectly. Too perfectly? Maybe.

That was why many fans will have been reining their excitement in.

The great thing for the players was they had a plan which asked a lot of them mentally and physically but which they trusted and which worked so well in the home draw with Tottenham and the win over Arsenal.

Effectively, it was to get in their faces.

Two months on to the day they clinched their famous win over the Gunners, they did it again.

Midfielder Dale Stephens said: "We went into the game full of confidence.

"We took confidence from the two

away games we had against them this year.

"The tempo was something that has probably worked against the likes of Arsenal and Tottenham, top teams.

"We have gone for a style where we get in their faces.

"It probably suits us as well. And the plan worked."

Pascal Gross, one of the quiet men of the team, looked around the home changing room and knew every man would have to defend like giants.

That included himself, the man who has been their most creative force.

The German playmaker said: "We first know we have to work very hard in our shape, everybody has to be ready to play defensively.

"If you win the ball you can play offensively but we have 11 defenders first and then we look forward and try to attack altogether.

"We played so hard in one-against-ones, we played high tempo."

Getting "in their faces" is not quite what it was.

The tackles don't fly in as in the old days.

Down under the giant West Stand, the players wait not in a cramped, intimidating narrow tunnel but in a

In your face, how Albion set about ruffling United

Dale Stephens gets in a tackle on Anthony Martial as Albion gave United no time to settle

spacious, modern holding area.

But the atmosphere was something special and they warmed to the task.

The stats show Albion made 19 tackles (it felt like more) to United's eight.

Bruno and Davy Propper got in five apiece and Stephens four.

United had almost 70% of possession but Albion had four on-target attempts to their three.

At half-time, the shots on target count read 3-0, a couple of them producing great saves by David De Gea.

And that does not include the bad miss by Shane Duffy with a header from a corner.

The one concern around the stands at half-time may well have been that Albion had not got their noses in front.

That was not shared in the changing room, Stephens revealed.

He said: "No, to be honest 0-0 at half-time against Man United is not a bad scoreline.

"We knew we would get a chance.

"It was probably fortuitous the

way it came but we will take that with the situation we are in.

"Staying up feels just as good as last year. It's like a promotion in itself.

"To secure Premier League football at the first time of asking is a big achievement for everyone associated with the club and we are hoping to build on what we have done this year and make a bigger statement.

"We can look around the changing room and be happy with what we have done."

Pascal Gross gets on the end of Jose Izquierdo's cross to direct his header home for the match winner Picture: Simon Dack

THE **GOAL**

By BRIAN OWEN
Albion reporter
brian.owen@theargus.co.uk

All about the desire as Gross rose to occasion

ALBION fans have seen Pascal Gross score with a header before.

But you would have to be a real stalwart, or Norfolk-based, to have seen it.

Gross admitted his headed winner against United was a rarity and put it down to bravery.

But he said it was not a total one-off.

Gross told The Argus: "Heading is not one of my strengths but I was brave in this moment and wanted to score and had the luck in the end.

"I haven't scored many with my head.

"In pre-season at Norwich I did but in a league game…"

Pundits were quick to pick up on the fact Gross was quicker, braver and more committed in getting to that cross by Jose Izquierdo.

Former Albion defender Matt Upson said: "It's all about the desire of Gross to win that header.

"It's nearly a great goal-line clearance by (Marcos) Rojo.

"Gross wanted it more. It's the only way the goal came.

"Gross made the run, he was on the move, he wanted that ball more."

In footballing parlance, the scorer 'gambled' when he thought the ball was coming across goal.

He said: "To be fair I speculated for something like that. You never know where the ball is coming.

"I was between the defenders and then hit the target with my header."

In the season when VAR came into English football, making its debut at the Amex, it will be goal-line technology which has marked Albion's campaign.

That clearance by Anthony Knockaert at the Bet365 Stadium when it seemed oxygen might be breathed into a Stoke revival by a late winner.

And now the 2.8cm by which Gross's header crossed the line.

Craig Pawson, Friday's referee, has been in the middle of uproar at the Amex before.

He was the referee targeted by furious fans for sending off Ashley Barnes and Romain Vincelot against Burnley in 2011.

This time the bedlam was of a more positive nature as, after that brief delay, they saw him pointing back to the centre circle.

As with VAR confirmation of Glenn Murray's winner against Crystal Palace in the FA Cup, the system worked smoothly, quickly and discreetly as it made sure justice was done.

Izquierdo's cross was diverted towards Gross by David De Gea and the Colombian was not credited with what would have been his fourth Premier League assist of the season.

But, this being United, there was an array of live TV coverage and pundits having their say.

Former Everton midfielder Peter Reid told Bein Sports viewers: "He does well to stand the ball up.

"It's a great, great cross from that position."

Reid added: "Brighton wanted it more."

Gross would agree with that.

The**PREM** »

Oscar leads accolades for Albion

KIND **WORDS**

JESSE LINGARD got into the best position to spoil Albion's shut-out.

And his former Albion boss was watching on television back home near Sabadell in Spain. Lingard played a neat one-two with Marcus Rashford but sidefooted wide as Shane Duffy slid in.

It was roles reversed from that previous Friday night season finale at the Amex four years ago, when Lingard scored for Albion and Yeovil defender Duffy was helpless.

"I watched it on TV at home," said Oscar Garcia (above), the man in charge when Lingard came on loan from United in the 2013-14 season.

"What did I think when he did the one-two? That he must have learnt a lot when he was on loan at Brighton" he said, jokingly.

Oscar was among the first to congratulate Albion on their win and staying up via social media. Elliott Bennett, who has helped Blackburn to promotion from League One, tweeted: "Brighton have been outstanding tonight. Knockaert taking liberties with United. All built on a massive foundation in Lewis Dunk and Shane Duffy. Been massive all season. Think Dunky will be knocking on the England door."

Bobby Zamora, who watched from right behind the Albion bench, hailed a "great win", Sebastien Pocognoli, the Standard Liege full-back who helped the Seagulls go up while on loan last season, tweeted: "Congratulations. Not surprised about that. Great job."

And ex-Seagulls defender Gary Stevens joked: "It's now vital that expectation for the 2018-19 season is controlled. I'm expecting only Europa League."

Shut-out brought up Ryan's top ten

CLEAN **SHEET**

By BRIAN OWEN
Albion reporter
brian.owen@theargus.co.uk

MATHEW RYAN took no chances as Albion hit their target of ten clean sheets for the season.

Not with his feet, nor with his hands when high balls came in.

Not even when Marcus Rashford sent in a shot which was not too far away but he pushed firmly to a wide position.

And not even long after the final whistle when he emerged to talk to the press.

"It's done now, yeah? We can't be caught?" he double, even triple-checked before speaking about the season.

Yes, it was done, thanks to a shut-out which always looked key to the win.

Albion legend Peter Ward had wished for "1-0 (Murray)" but "1-0 (Gross)" was just as perfect.

United are the only team this season to have won every Premier League game in which they have scored first, 20 in all.

Albion have taken just three points after going behind.

So the nil meant so much and Albion did not have too many scares along the way.

Ryan said: "As a group we set a number of goals in a number of aspects of the game, statistics and what not, and ten clean sheets was one of them.

"I thought we were well on track for that at one stage.

"It was a bit disappointing from Newcastle to Burnley it took almost four months to get that following one.

"To get two in a row is huge."

Albion are one of ten teams to be in double figures for clean sheets.

They have kept five at home and five away but their most recent at the Amex had been just before Christmas against Watford.

Ryan, whose late penalty save at Stoke was one of the key moments of the season, believes the Seagulls have learnt a lot, sometimes the hard way.

No alarms for Mathew Ryan against Man United

He said: "There are always lessons within games – game management, reading of the play, moments in matches.

"When you get to a level like this the speed is a lot quicker, players are a lot smarter, players are a lot more skilful, you have to adapt to that and across the board I think we have been doing that throughout the season.

"I really feel like we have made a lot of progress as a team."

Ryan tends to exude a sense of calm and he says that was also the case over recent weeks as he found himself in a new situation.

He didn't take his work home with him too often, even when the drop zone was not far away.

The former Valencia and Club Brugge goalkeeper added: "I have been lucky enough to win a couple of trophies up to now and it is the best feeling in the world.

"It's the first time in my career I've been involved in a relegation fight a little bit.

"No one wishes for that but that's the nature of the Premier League.

"There are no easy games and I think it is a lot more fun playing for titles than playing for survival You have got a little bit more to lose."

But did he worry at all about going down?

"Yes, probably. But I take one game at a time and wasn't really thinking too much.

"I was just living in the moment and trying to do my best each week to contribute to getting safe.

"Because of the closeness of it, there is always that thought every now and then about if we were to go down.

"But I was quite confident we had the personnel, the infrastructure and everything around us to stay up and we have managed to do that for next season."

True lap of honour for Albion squad

IT LOOKS like a lap of honour but usually it isn't.

It is called a lap of thanks or appreciation and it is a chance for fans and players to say goodbye at the end of the season.

Albion players and their families walked around behind painted smiles after the home defeat by Bristol City last season.

There was an underwhelmed feel after the 1-1 draw with Derby two years ago, although the North Stand tried to lift spirits by chanting "we are going up".

And it was a bit like glad it's all over when 2014-15 ended.

Not this time. It was thanks, appreciation – and, indeed, honour.

There are players who have not played but who are valued for their input around the club.

Others who have striven to get into the side and kept those ahead of them on their toes.

Bruno himself fitted into that latter category for a few weeks.

The skipper said: "Thank you to all those players who haven't been playing all season or just training, helping us. They are so important."

He told fans over the microphone: "After I think one of the best games at the Amex, thanks so much to the fans for the support. Without you it would not be possible."

Ezequiel Schelotto, the man who has shared right-back duties with Bruno, was among those enjoying himself.

He gave exhausted winger Jose Izquierdo a lift and joined his fellow Latin American in song (below). The two have become inseparable since teaming up in August.

"Only you and me know what we were singing," Schelotto later tweeted.

Amex lap of honour for the Seagulls players and families

That last effort was 'something special'

By BRIAN OWEN
Albion reporter
brian.owen@theargus.co.uk

AS THAT precious win loomed closer, Albion fans and players raised their game again.

And nowhere was that noticed more keenly than high in the West Stand, where chairman Tony Bloom was loving, and living, every moment.

Bloom and chief executive Paul Barber were celebrating in the aisles after Pascal Gross scored.

But it was in that final push that they really felt something special going on around them on what might just have been the greatest night at the Amex.

The noise was deafening, the atmosphere intimidating and the buzz intoxicating as safety, secured

END **GAME**

in the grand manner, loomed large.

Barber and Bloom relished the way the crowd empathised with what was going on as their team were pushed back.

And how they roared them through what became a case of attack versus defence – with defence not giving an inch.

Barber said: "The support from the fans late in the match was incredible.

"It was on a par with the Sheffield Wednesday play-off which we so often talk about, particularly in that last part.

"It was a sign we have something special going on.

"A point would have been fine. Three points were what everybody

from the fans to the players and ourselves wanted.

"We wanted that special night and everybody came together at the right time.

"I think the fans sensed what the players needed from them.

"The fans created that forcefield once again to help stop Manchester United scoring."

Albion have used the word 'together' a lot in the past three seasons, often accompanied by a hashtag.

Barber accepts they have hammered that one home.

He said: "Everybody came together in a way in which we have almost demanded in the last few years."

The Albion directors sit with their families in the best seats in the West Stand, Barber a few rows in front of the chairman.

They soaked it up as bedlam con-

tinued around them. Barber said: "Tony has invested so much financially and emotionally into this club.

"People talk a lot about the financial side but you should also see the sheer emotion he puts into the club.

"No chairman in the Premier League has quite that emotional attachment expect maybe Dean Hoyle at Huddersfield and perhaps one or two others.

"Friday night meant a huge amount to him.

"When we scored we were in the aisles like a couple of teenagers at a pop concert.

"I think other directors look at him a bit surprised at times.

"We celebrate our goals like fans. If you can't celebrate a goal, what are you doing there. We do so as well away from home, without being disrespectful to the home club."